**New Directions for
Child and Adolescent
Development**

Reed W. Larson
Lene Arnett Jensen
EDITORS-IN-CHIEF

William Damon
FOUNDING EDITOR

The Intersections of Personal and Social Identities

Margarita Azmitia
Moin Syed
Kimberley Radmacher
EDITORS

D1523390

Number 120 • Summer 2008
Jossey-Bass
San Francisco

THE INTERSECTIONS OF PERSONAL AND SOCIAL IDENTITIES
Margarita Azmitia, Moin Syed, Kimberley Radmacher (eds.)
New Directions for Child and Adolescent Development, no. 120
Reed W. Larson, Lene Arnett Jensen, Editors-in-Chief

Microfilm copies of issues and articles are available in 16mm and 35mm,
as well as microfiche in 105mm, through University Microfilms, Inc.,
300 North Zeeb Road, Ann Arbor, Michigan 48106-1346.

ISSN 1520-3247   electronic ISSN 1534-8687

NEW DIRECTIONS FOR CHILD AND ADOLESCENT DEVELOPMENT is part of The
Jossey-Bass Education Series and is published quarterly by Wiley Sub-
scription Services, Inc., a Wiley company, at Jossey-Bass, 989 Market
Street, San Francisco, California 94103-1741. Periodicals postage paid at
San Francisco, California, and at additional mailing offices. Postmaster:
Send address changes to New Directions for Child and Adolescent Devel-
opment, Jossey-Bass, 989 Market Street, San Francisco, CA 94103-1741.

New Directions for Child and Adolescent Development is indexed in Cam-
bridge Scientific Abstracts (CSA/CIG), CHID: Combined Health Infor-
mation Database (NIH), Contents Pages in Education (T&F), Current
Abstracts (EBSCO), Educational Research Abstracts Online (T&F),
ERIC Database (Education Resources Information Center), Index
Medicus/MEDLINE/PubMed (NLM), Linguistics & Language Behavior
Abstracts (CSA/CIG), Psychological Abstracts/PsycINFO (APA), Social
Services Abstracts (CSA/CIG), SocINDEX (EBSCO), and Sociological
Abstracts (CSA/CIG).

SUBSCRIPTION rates: For the U.S., $85 for individuals and $258 for institutions. Please see ordering information page at end of journal.

EDITORIAL CORRESPONDENCE should be e-mailed to the editors-in-chief:
Reed W. Larson (larsonr@uiuc.edu) and Lene Arnett Jensen (ljensen@
clarku.edu).

Jossey-Bass Web address: www.josseybass.com

CONTENTS

Azmitia, M., Syed, M., & Radmacher, K. (2008). On the intersection of personal and social identities: Introduction and evidence from a longitudinal study of emerging adults. In M. Azmitia, M. Syed, & K. Radmacher (Eds.), *The intersections of personal and social identities. New Directions for Child and Adolescent Development, 120*, 1–16.

1

On the Intersection of Personal and Social Identities: Introduction and Evidence from a Longitudinal Study of Emerging Adults

Margarita Azmitia, Moin Syed, Kimberley Radmacher

Abstract

Identity is a central focus of research in the social sciences, national and international politics, and everyday discourse. This volume brings together an interdisciplinary set of social scientists who study personal and social identity. The chapters span childhood through emerging adulthood. This chapter introduces

Our longitudinal study of diverse emerging adults' college pathways was funded by grants from the Academic Senate and Social Sciences Division of the University of California at Santa Cruz (UCSC), UC-ACCORD and UC-LMRI, and the Spencer Foundation. We are grateful to the university's Educational Opportunity Programs and admissions office for help with recruiting participants and William Ladusaw, the provosts of the ten colleges at UCSC, and Mary Ann Dewey from UCSC's public information office for help locating participants during and after their time at UCSC. We thank Catherine R. Cooper, Lene Jensen, and Avril Thorne for providing insightful feedback on earlier versions of the chapter and all the colleagues and students who helped with the research and who have patiently listened to the ideas that helped frame this volume and our research.

the three goals of the volume: (1) illustrating how the study of identity develop-
ment is enriched by an interdisciplinary approach, (2) providing a rich devel-
opmental picture of personal and social identity development, and (3) examining
the intersections of multiple identities. We illustrate these three goals with brief
descriptions of how they are addressed in the other chapters in the volume. This
chapter also highlights the three goals of the study with data from our ongoing
longitudinal study of diverse emerging adults' college pathways. © Wiley Periodicals, Inc.

> Whenever Richard Cory went down town,
> We people on the pavement looked at him:
> He was a gentleman from sole to crown,
> Clean favored, and imperially slim.
>
> And he was always quietly arrayed,
> And he was always human when he talked;
> But still he fluttered pulses when he said,
> "Good-morning," and he glittered when he walked.
>
> And he was rich—yes, richer than a king,
> And admirably schooled in every grace:
> In fine, we thought that he was everything
> To make us wish that we were in his place.
>
> So on we worked, and waited for the light,
> And went without the meat, and cursed the bread;
> And Richard Cory, one calm summer night
> Went home and put a bullet through his head.
>
> Edwin Arlington Robinson

Richard Cory. Silvia Plath. Edgar Allan Poe. Virginia Woolf. Anne Sex-
ton. Ernest Hemingway. Adolescents or emerging adults who are on
suicide watch at the local mental health facility or, like Richard Cory,
appeared to all their family, friends, and teachers to have everything going for
them and yet were found dead, with only a note left behind (or not) about
why they could not go on. The war veterans who come home but are lost
because after the atrocities they have seen or done in the name of their country, religion, or any group that is part of their identity, home no longer is
home. The list could go on, but this inability to see one's past, present, and
future as coherent and meaningful was what sparked Erik Erikson's interest
in identity development, his greatest life and scholarly passion.

When Erikson started writing about identity as a result of trying to help
World War II veterans recover their sense of self through crafting a life story
that integrated the past, present and future, the current clinical name for
this incoherence of the self, posttraumatic stress disorder (PTSD), had not
been invented. Subsequently Erikson traveled to California to study the
Sioux and other Native American nations. In his interviews with parents

and grandparents, Erikson discovered a similar issue of incoherence of self in the children of these nations and theorized that this incoherence was in large part due to the U.S. government's practice of sending children to boarding schools where they were essentially cut off from their cultural roots. When these children rejoined their families, they had become different people who no longer felt at home in their community and often had not found home at the boarding school either. Today Erikson's ideas about the basic human need for self-coherence and the association between coherence and mental health are still timely and the focus of many scholarly and applied endeavors, as is his unwavering interest in examining how cultural communities either constrain or facilitate self-exploration.

Since Erikson's landmark book, *Identity: Youth and Crisis* (1968), on the uses and misuses of the term *identity* in psychology, the general public, and various cultural institutions, developmental psychologists have theorized and researched the various meanings of personal identity in children, adolescents, and, more recently, adults. Increased globalization has made identity development even more challenging. Currently, children, adolescents, and adults in even the most remote corners of the world have instant access to media. Thus, the boundaries and contexts for identity development have been broadened to include multiple choices and pathways through development. With choices, however, often comes confusion, making identity crafting more challenging. Fortunately, cultural communities, families, peers, and schools set up scaffolds to guide identity exploration toward the goals, values, beliefs, and practices associated with mature identities in their communities. Still, some confusion is bound to occur as young children and adults move toward a more mature understanding of their role in their communities and in the larger, and at times very different, globalized world that children, adolescents, and emerging adults find themselves in.

One such confusion is whether a person's unique, or personal, self develops in connection with his or her sense of belonging to a group or collective (social) identity. The intersection of personal and social identities is receiving increasing attention in a variety of disciplines: education, sociology, and developmental, personality, and social psychology. In developmental psychology, for example, the study of personal identity has been dominated by Eriksonian (1968) and neo-Eriksonian approaches, and in particular, Marcia's identity status model. (Erikson did not use the term *personal identity* in his writings. He would also have disagreed with Tajfel's (1981) proposal that personal and social identities are separable. See Cooper, Behrens, & Trinh, in press.)

More recently, autobiographical narrative approaches, which are rooted in personality psychology (McAdams, 2001; Thorne, 2004), have begun to capture the dynamic instantiations of adolescents' and adults' identities. Both approaches are consistent with Erikson's proposal that personal identity is an individual project that engages with historical, cultural, and social contexts and practices (see also Penuel & Wertsch, 1995; Thorne, 2004). Following Erikson, both approaches posit that the optimal developmental outcome for adolescents and adults is to achieve a sense of coherence that integrates their multiple identifications across contexts and time. This conceptualization does not preclude variations in the contextual salience of identity, but it does suggest that individuals will have a sense of "me-ness" or continuity across various contexts.

In contrast, variations in identity across different contexts have been the primary focus of social psychologists. Influenced by social identity theory (Ashmore, Deaux, & McLaughlin-Volpe, 2004; Tajfel & Turner, 1986), social psychologists have examined social identity rather than personal identity, defined by Tajfel (1981) as "that part of an individual's self-concept which derives from his knowledge of his membership of a social group together with the value and emotional significance attached to that membership" (p. 63). Therefore, as opposed to a unique, individual sense of "me-ness" that defines personal identity, social identity involves collective, group-level identification that represents a sense of "we-ness" (Ruble et al., 2004). (For a more extensive review of Tajfel's social identity theory, see Hurtado and Silva, Chapter Two.)

To date, researchers have typically investigated personal and social identities in relative isolation. However, there have recently been attempts to link together personal and social identities (see, for example, Deaux & Perkins, 2001; Phinney, 1990; Fuligni & Flook, 2005; Ruble et al., 2004). Deaux and Perkins (2001) used the metaphor of a kaleidoscope to illustrate how the fluidity and salience of individuals' personal, social, and relational identities depend on the situational context and provide multiple lenses for interpreting their experiences. The addition of the relational self—the everyday roles and dyadic relationships through which individuals enact and create their personal and social identities—to the kaleidoscope provides the added benefit of examining the inherent status hierarchies embedded in most roles and relationships and allows the investigation of how these hierarchies inform individuals' personal and social identities in their everyday lives. Unfortunately, although Deaux and Perkins's model provides a powerful metaphor that links personal and social identities, it has not been elaborated in sufficient detail to be tested empirically. As Thorne (2004) noted, "One of the biggest challenges for identity research is to achieve a dynamic and contextualized understanding of how senses of self are continuous *and* changing, and how personal *and* community beliefs and practices intertwine in identity making" (p. 5).

In this volume, we bring together identity scholars from multiple disciplines who offer new insights into the development of personal and social identities. As Jean Phinney suggests in her commentary on the contributions to this volume (Chapter Seven), we recognize that much work will be required to create a truly interdisciplinary approach to the study of identity development.

The three overarching goals of this volume are to (1) illustrate how the study of identity development is enriched by an interdisciplinary approach, (2) provide a rich developmental perspective or story about personal and social identity from childhood to emerging adulthood, and (3) examine the intersections of multiple identities. The chapters focus on the development of gender, ethnicity, and social class identities because these three social identities stratify most cultural communities. The chapter authors also address, to varying extents, how societal institutions—family, peers, schools, and media—contour the development of personal and social identities and shape educational and work/career trajectories. Phinney discusses whether and how each chapter addresses the three goals and suggests important directions for future research. To not steal her thunder, we will not fore-shadow her ideas in this introduction.

In this first chapter, we elaborate on the three goals of the volume in two ways. First, as we discuss each goal, we provide illustrations of how the chapter authors address each theme. Second, to provide a more in-depth analysis of each goal, we show how it framed our four-year longitudinal study of ethnically and socioeconomically diverse emerging adults' transition to and pathways through college. Our longitudinal study was initially motivated by our desire to help understand shared and unique experiences of students who are well represented (such as those of European and Asian heritage) and underrepresented (those of Chicano/Latino, African, Pacific Islander, and Native American heritage) in the undergraduate student body of the University of California (UC), and more specifically, our own campus: University of California at Santa Cruz. We also included a group of first-generation, low-income, European-heritage students to attempt to uncouple the roles of social class and ethnicity in our participants' college pathways.

In addition to our scholarly interest in this group of college students, we were motivated by the practical goal of increasing retention of these underrepresented students at UC. Thus, we worked closely with campus centers and organizations that serve these populations and routinely informed them of our emerging findings so they could make our campus friendlier to their constituents. As the study progressed, identity development began to take a more central role in our scholarly and practical interests because our participants' college narratives were not only about adapting to and managing academics and social activities at the campus. As participants progressed through their four or more years toward graduation, they were creating identity narratives that integrated their past, present, and future values, beliefs, goals, and cultural practices.

The Goals of the Volume

We now turn to how the authors and our work addressed the three goals of the volume: interdisciplinarity, identity development, and the intersections or connections between identities.

Interdisciplinarity in the Study of Personal and Social Identity. Like other disciplines, developmental psychology has benefited from interdisciplinary and postmodern approaches to identity theory and research. Following Marxist and feminist theorists' ideas about positioning (Harding, 2004), as

NEW DIRECTIONS FOR CHILD AND ADOLESCENT DEVELOPMENT • DOI: 10.1002/cd

well as the ideas of Bourdieu (1977) and Coleman (1988) about the role of social capital in educational and career opportunities, developmental psychologists have increasingly recognized that because of their gender, ethnicity, and social class, some children, adolescents, and emerging adults have more opportunities than others to explore and construct their educational and career identities. These stratifying demographic categories also influence these groups' ideas about relationships and their political and moral ideologies. Thus, as sociologists and social psychologists have long argued, these social identities should be included in theory and research on personal identity development. As the chapters in this volume illustrate, scholars focused on social identity development would also benefit from attention to personal identity development.

The chapter authors illustrate how drawing on a variety of disciplinary theories can increase our understanding of identity development. In addition to their theoretical plurality, the interdisciplinary approach of the contributors is evident in their research methods. Because the intersection of personal and social identities is complex and multifaceted, the methods used are necessarily diverse, making use of quantitative, interview, narrative, ethnographic, focus group, and content-analytic approaches. In particular, Aída Hurtado and Janelle Silva (Chapter Two, social psychologists and feminist scholars), Leah Lurye, Kristina Zosuls, and Diane Ruble (Chapter Three, developmental and social psychologists), Lyn Mikel Brown and Mark Tappan (Chapter Four, developmental and educational psychologists), Niobe Way, Carlos Santos, Erika Niwa, and Constance Kim-Gervey (Chapter Five, developmental psychologists), Mark Orbe (Chapter Six, a sociologist), and Jean Phinney (Chapter Seven, a developmental psychologist) drew on theory and research in social and developmental psychology, sociology, education, anthropology, feminist studies, and philosophy to create their conceptual frameworks and formulate their theoretical proposals, research questions, and data analyses. Except for Lurye, Zosuls, and Ruble, who used a quantitative approach, the contributors to this volume privileged qualitative methods in their analysis of personal and social identities. However, an examination of the authors' published works shows that depending on their particular theoretical issue or research questions, they move fluidly through a variety of methods and data analytic techniques.

Interdisciplinarity in Our Own Research. Our longitudinal study recruited 175 ethnically and socioeconomically diverse women and men who entered our University of California's campus in fall 2002. The approximately 100 students who remained at the university until their senior year (2006) are the focus of this chapter. Our project drew heavily from theories and methods in social psychology, education, feminist theory, and sociology. Our conception of personal identity was greatly influenced by Cooper's (1999) interdisciplinary bridging multiple worlds theory, which emphasizes identity negotiation among young people's salient personal contexts or worlds, such as families, peers, schools, and communities, and how these worlds can serve as both resources and challenges for their identity formation and career pathways. The first-generation participants—students who were the first in their families to attend college—often poignantly illustrated these resources and constraints in our longitudinal study. For example, many talked about attending underresourced public schools in dangerous neighborhoods and persisting in school despite many obstacles to fulfill their parents' dreams that their children would go to college and escape poverty. What they lacked in family academic credentials, or human capital, they often made up in emotional support from family, friends, and, for some, teachers and community- and school-based organizations. (Human capital is conceptualized in our research as parents' educational level and their families' familiarity with U.S. schools, requirements for university admission, and generally U.S. universities and college degrees.) A few students, however, saw themselves as their most important source of capital for negotiating and navigating college, identity, and their futures (see also Cooper, Cooper, Azmitia, Chavira, & Gullat, 2002).

We used social identity theory (Tajfel & Turner, 1986) and standpoint theory (Harding, 2004) to explore how our participants negotiated their gender, ethnic, and social class identities within the multiple contexts of personal identity. We were especially interested in whether and how they came to understand how these social identities positioned them in college and in the broader society. For example, many of the participants who had at least one subordinate identity (for example, female, ethnic minority, or poor or working class) were surprised to encounter prejudice and racism at the university, a place they had always equated with democratic policies and beliefs. Dominant group members, in contrast, often disclosed the guilt or powerlessness they felt when they first encountered notions of privilege in their university classrooms or in interactions with peers. As they went through college, subordinate- and dominant-group emerging adults attempted to understand each other's positioning—where the "other" was coming from—and how this positioning informed their own identity negotiations and development. We would argue that our participants' willingness to work to understand their own and others' positioning helped them recognize and articulate connections between their personal and social identities and construct increasingly coherent identity narratives.

Personal and Social Identity Development from Childhood to Emerging Adulthood. Although Erikson (1968) argued that identity development is a lifelong project that begins in infancy, theory and research on identity development have typically been located in adolescence. Recently Arnett (2004) and many others have highlighted the dramatic changes that have taken place in adolescents' and adults' lives in many postindustrial communities. As a result, they have made a compelling case that the negotiation of identity extends beyond adolescence and into emerging adulthood, a transitional phase between adolescence and young adulthood. At the same time, others (Quintana, 2007; Ruble et al., 2004) have highlighted the importance of identity formation in childhood. Accordingly, this volume includes work that spans early childhood through emerging adulthood. In this way, we hope to highlight similarities and differences in identity formation across developmental periods.

As the chapter authors argue, although gender, ethnicity, and social class are integral parts of people's lives, the salience and centrality of these social identities vary as a function of period of development (childhood, adolescence, or emerging adulthood) and the life contexts they inhabit. Following Tajfel and Turner (1986), several researchers have shown that individuals who occupy less privileged positions in their cultural communities by virtue of their demographic group memberships, women, people of color, and the working class or poor in the United States and other nations are more aware of their social identities than individuals who occupy more privileged positions (for example, white middle- or upper-class males). The heightened awareness or salience of these social identities is fueled by experiences of discrimination and socially imposed constraints in their daily lives. Yet the research also shows that being a member of these groups (for example, being female) does not automatically imply that a particular social identity is meaningful to the child, adolescent, or emerging adult (see also Chapters Two and Three). Still, because identities are created and negotiated in social contexts, others may impose identities on individuals based on assumptions concerning the salience or centrality of that identity for the individual (see also Chapters Four through Six). The interesting developmental questions then become: When and how do these social identities develop? What accounts for between- and within-group variation in the centrality of these social identities in children's, adolescents', and emerging adults' identity projects? When and how do individuals begin to link their social and their personal identities? Do they perceive these linkages as kaleidoscopic lenses or positions for negotiating their lives? We asked the chapter authors to grapple with these four questions as they wrote their chapters.

We also asked the chapter authors to consider how personal and social identities are socialized, created, and performed in relational and institutional contexts such as family, peers, schools, and media. Way, Santos, Niwa, and Kim-Gervey (Chapter Five) and Orbe (Chapter Six) highlight the role of family, peers, and schools in personal and social identity development. As Hurtado and Silva (Chapter Two) and Brown and Tappan (Chapter Four) remind us, media also exert a powerful influence on identity negotiations. Yet as Lurye, Zosuls, and Ruble (Chapter Three) caution, families, peers, schools, media, and, more broadly, cultural communities exert their influence through individuals' personal identity lenses, and these lenses can lead to individual differences in identity constructions, with implications for adjustment and mental health.

Personal and Social Identity Development in Our Own Research. We now show how our longitudinal study of diverse emerging adults' college pathways addressed the four developmental questions we asked contributors to ponder in the context of family, peer, and institutional (college) worlds. Using examples from the participants' interviews, we highlight how emerging adults' social identities contextualized our participants' educational trajectories and career identities, two domains of personal identity development. We draw attention to the processes of identity negotiation, including the triggers and personal characteristics that either enhanced or hindered the salience, centrality, and integration of our participants' social and personal identities. Although we included narratives from a broad range of participants, we pay special attention to the stories of first-generation college students because they experienced the most discontinuities between their precollege and college lives (see also Chapter Six), and these discontinuities often served as potential triggers for personal and social identity development.

During their first year of college, our participants varied in the extent to which they had formulated career goals and could articulate their motivation for attending college. They also varied in the salience and centrality of their gender, ethnic, and social class identities for interpreting the academic and social experiences they were encountering as they began and adjusted to college life. Although students who were members of subordinate groups (ethnic minorities, females, and poor and working-class students) were more likely to mention these social identities, many denied that these identities played a role in their major or career choices. For example, Rose, a working-class Chinese American student, stated that ethnicity was not related to her career choices because "I just never let it get to me, I never really thought of ethnicity as a big deal. We're all people, human beings." She had similar feelings about gender and social class. This denial that social identities mattered for a domain of personal identity, career, may have occurred at least in part because first-year students generally viewed college as an equalizer that would erase their disadvantaged status in society.

As they experienced college, however, first-generation students began to understand that college reproduced the inequalities in the larger society and that these social identities would contour their experiences and choices throughout their lives (see Chapter Two). For many, this understanding led to an increased salience and centrality of gender, ethnicity, or class in their identity narratives and career pathways. For example, although she expressed similar ideas to Rose in the fall quarter of her first year, the winter and spring quarter interviews showed that Ana, a working-class Latina, was beginning to see connections among her ethnicity, career, and, more broadly, her life. Taking a course in American studies appears to have triggered this awareness: "It's like, about race and just seeing the world totally different, and like, books that like, I read in high school and now that I read here, I was like, 'Whoa; it's totally different!' Like, you totally get a different meaning to it." Taking this course also seems to have been the catalyst in her change of major and career, although she gave her personal dislike of chemistry as her primary reason for switching her major from chemistry to sociology.

Our participants' sophomore year interviews revealed a gradual increase in making connections among personal (career) and social identities.

However, many still struggled with the tension between viewing their choices exclusively as self-determined and recognizing that these choices were influenced at least in part by their gender, ethnic, and social class. In Ana's sophomore year, for example, sociology remained her major because "I really like it. I like the concepts. I took a class and now it's just like, you know what this is what I want to do. . . . I'm not really thinking about 'I'm a minority, I want to study this for minorities.'" Yet in a subsequent section of this narrative, she stated that her ethnicity had influenced her goal of becoming a lawyer because "just me being a minority, there isn't that many minorities that are lawyers."

For a handful of sophomores, however, their college experiences, choice of majors, and social identities were intimately connected and viewed as microcosms of how U.S. society marks gender, ethnicity, social class, and other social identities. Robert, a working-class African American student from an inner-city neighborhood who was the only one of his friends who attended college, repeatedly stressed how he viewed his college experiences from his ethnic, gender, and class positions because "society just puts you in a box. . . . If I were to forget that I was Black one day, I would always be reminded every time I, like, step outside, get on the bus, and [am] like, kinda a spectacle all the time. . . . It's hard to decipher whether a girl is looking at you because she likes you or because you are Black." Robert also explained that he had majored in economics because this major was both interesting to him and would allow him to have a career that paid enough for him to help his family and community. Yet he stated that he was finding it increasingly difficult to visit his family and friends as he created an upwardly mobile, college student identity because neither his friends nor his family understood his college experiences (see also Chapter Six). Despite these challenges, his interviews showed that his commitment to his family, friends, and community never wavered from his first through his senior years.

Like Erikson (1968), social scientists have suggested that particular experiences may serve as triggers (Phinney, 2003) or encounters (Cross, 1995) that prompt identity exploration and renegotiation (see also Chapter Two). Narrative life story theorists have suggested that the processes through which individuals make meaning of their experiences also play a role in the extent to which identities are explored, negotiated, and renegotiated (Thorne, 2004). The relation between people's experiences and social and personal identity development is bidirectional in that experiences and opportunities help create particular identities and particular identities will seek out or be afforded particular experiences and opportunities. It is important to note that these triggers are not universally applicable; for example, finding that one is a numerical minority on the college campus, experiencing racism or discrimination from a peer or a professor, or traveling to one's ancestral culture will not prompt identity work for everyone. The same or similar experiences can have different effects on different people, and this differential impact may be related to their current construction of their social or personal identity, including their personality traits, motives, and concerns.

NEW DIRECTIONS FOR CHILD AND ADOLESCENT DEVELOPMENT • DOI: 10.1002/cd

In our longitudinal study, we found that consistent with prior research, experiences of racism and discrimination were especially powerful triggers for identity work. Our participants were often unsettled by these experiences and discussed them with their friends and family as they tried to make sense of them. Of course, triggers for identity development were not limited to experiences of prejudice. For example, in his senior-year interview, Robert stated that his participation in Rainbow Theater (a multicultural, multiethnic theater group on campus) had affirmed his pride in his African American and working-class heritage and promoted an understanding of and tolerance for other groups. Our key point is that the college context offers a wide array of potential experiences that may cause emerging adults to rethink their identities and reconfigure them in new ways.

University courses frequently served as consciousness-raising experiences for our participants (see also Chapter Two), including students from privileged groups who were confronting issues of privilege and subordination for the first time. For some, the increased salience of their privileged gender, ethnicity, or class position not only triggered identity work but also prompted them to become involved in activities such as pro-immigration rallies, labor strikes, the annual take-back-the-night march, and on-campus and community organizations working for social change.

Interactions with peers outside the classroom also triggered identity work, particularly for college students living away from home. Rose's senior-year interview was characterized by an increased salience and centrality of her ethnic (Chinese) identity following a quarter studying abroad in Hong Kong, where she met a Chinese American student who was actively involved with her ethnicity. This trip to Hong Kong was clearly a turning point for her ethnic identity, and identity development in general. In describing her behavior since she returned, Rose said: "[I'm more] aware of my own ethnicity. Aware of if something goes on or someone says something to me, I'm like 'oh, maybe they said it because I'm Asian.' Like, well, my first couple weeks coming back, over the summer when I came back, a lot of my friends noticed that I made more racial remarks, racial comments."

Rose's description of her behavior is illustrative of what we have previously referred to as an ethnic lens (Syed & Azmitia, in press), such that she now views events and experiences in terms of her ethnicity, a behavior that we found corresponds to a greater identification with one's ethnic group (see also Cross, 1995) and is associated with the increased salience and centrality of particular identities in emerging adults' identity projects. Taken together with the excerpts from Rose's other interviews we quoted earlier, this comment also suggests that Rose is beginning to appreciate the connections or intersections between her personal and social identities.

The Intersectionality of Personal and Social Identities. The connections between individuals' multiple identities have been conceptualized in three ways. As discussed by scholars from critical race theory (Dixson & Rousseau, 2005), feminists of Color (hooks, 2003; Hurtado & Silva,

NEW DIRECTIONS FOR CHILD AND ADOLESCENT DEVELOPMENT • DOI: 10.1002/cd

Chapter Two, this volume), and social scientists interested in multicultural education (Waters, 1996), intersectionality concerns individuals' positioning in their cultural communities and the broader society. Focusing primarily on race and class (critical race theory) and race and gender (feminist studies), these scholars reject a hierarchical, or additive, approach to social identities. Rather, they have emphasized how social identities intersect to create unique positions within society; because these identities all work together to shape experiences, they cannot be understood in isolation. For example, although by virtue of their gender Black and white female students can experience similar gender-related challenges and resources in their career pathways, their experiences will be inherently unique because their ethnicity puts them in either a subordinate or dominant position at the university and in society. In this example, Black female students potentially experience two intersecting systems of oppression (gender and race), and white females potentially experience only one system of oppression (gender).

All of the chapter authors address this structural conceptualization of intersectionality to some degree. Hurtado and Silva, for example, illustrate how the creators of the *Little Bill* TV series interweave positive messages about ethnicity, gender, disability, and to an extent, social class, in their episode "A Ramp for Monty." In their discussion of gender identity development, Lurye, Zosuls, and Ruble and Brown and Tappan illustrate the importance of considering the complex interconnections among sex typing, centrality, typicality, and power for understanding not only gender identity development but also the association between gender identity and mental health. Intersectionality is also illustrated by Way, Santos, Niwa, and Kim-Gervey in their analyses of how late adolescents create connections among ethnicity, gender, class, nationality, and other social identities in the context of their high school, and in Orbe's discussion of how ethnic majority and minority poor and working-class first-generation college students negotiate the dialectical tensions between their peer interactions in their university and home communities.

The second sense of how intersectionality has been conceptualized in the literature is akin to Erikson's (1968) ideas about the importance of coherence for identity development. In this framing, intersectionality refers to the integration (or nonintegration) of individuals' multiple selves, relationships, and worlds (see, for example, Cooper, 1999; Harter, 1999). This approach to intersectionality is illustrated particularly well in Orbe's discussion of how first-generation college students negotiate the dialectical tension between the identities they perform with family and friends in their home communities and the upwardly mobile identities they perform with peers and professors at the university.

Within developmental psychology, the third and final approach to intersectionality concerns statistical interactions between age and personal and social identities. For example, as Hurtado and Silva noted, research on personal and social identity development has consistently highlighted the role of cognitive skills in the complexity of children, adolescents, and emerging adults' personal and social identities and their ability. Lurye, Zosuls, and Ruble convincingly show how the nature of the statistical interaction of sex typing, gender identity, and adjustment differs in early and late middle childhood.

Intersectionality in Emerging Adulthood: Evidence from Our Longitudinal Study. The most striking finding from our longitudinal analysis of our participants' identity narratives was their increasing ability to articulate the connections among their multiple identities. Typically during their first year, participants discussed the domains of personal and social identity we studied in relative isolation even when prompted by interview questions to discuss the connections between them. Such was not the case in their senior-year interviews, when most spontaneously made these connections. For example, during her first-year interviews, Rose denied that her ethnicity, gender, or social class played a role in her life. In contrast, during her senior-year interview, she frequently discussed the intersection between her ethnic and gender identities. She told us repeatedly that being a Chinese female was a source of challenge in her family and that this challenge affected her ability to focus on her major and career. She narrated several experiences to support her views, such as when her brother received a "full ride" to college from her parents but she had to work to help pay for her own tuition and living expenses. However, Rose's narratives did not articulate a very sophisticated view about how these social identities contextualized her career identity or her position in the larger society. She also viewed identity largely as a personal project and not as a something that affects the groups she identified with.

In contrast, in her senior-year interview, Ana made more complex connections among her experiences, social identities, and her career choices (a domain of personal identity). She believed her gender would be a challenge because law is male dominated, but that her ethnicity would be an asset because of the perceived need for diversity in the judicial system. An examination of Ana's first- through senior-year interviews showed that trying to make sense of experiences of racism and discrimination increased her understanding of the intersections between her social identities. At the beginning of her first year of college, she distanced herself from others in her ethnic group when she described her parents' support of her attending college: "I'm going to college. I'm trying harder. In my culture that's good, because people usually settle for less. And I think that's helped me because I don't settle for less." In her sophomore year, Ana aligned herself with her ethnic group and began to see the intersection of ethnicity and social class after an experience of prejudice in which a middle-class white acquaintance accused Ana's Latina friend of "spending my parents' tax money on your digital camera" because Ana's friend had used part of her financial aid to pay for the camera. Ana expressed her frustration in the conflation of class and race that permeates our society, her understanding that others might perceive her differently because of her social class, and her resolve to prove these stereotypes wrong. This experience did not affect "how I view myself, but I guess how other people might view me. Because of however much your parents make." Moments later when asked about which social identity was most salient and central to her, she said ethnicity, "because people are always classifying people by what you are."

Ana's more complex understanding of the intersections between class and ethnicity included the realization that her social class was viewed as a stereotype of her ethnicity and therefore made her ethnicity more salient to others. This was a common sentiment among the participants regarding the intersection of class and ethnicity: the working-class Asian American and white emerging adult participants stated that they were often viewed as middle class, whereas the Latino and African American participants stated that others frequently assumed they were from poor or working-class backgrounds. Ana's narrative also reflects the challenges of creating intersections between one's identities and the ambivalence that can result from this process. Although Ana recognized that her ethnicity and social class identities were inherently connected, she still wished that society would not conflate ethnicity and social class.

Our emerging adult participants' understanding of their social and personal identities and the intersections between them was also mediated by their personal agency in seeking out experiences of diversity. For example, Leslie, a white working-class female who viewed social class as her most salient social identity, actively sought out experiences that would broaden her appreciation of and tolerance for diversity. As illustrated by her narrative of an experience in her legal studies class when they discussed *Brown v. Board of Education of Topeka, Kansas,* these experiences allowed her to begin to articulate the intersection of her identities. In the lead-in narrative to the following quotation, she stated that her predominantly white home community and high school were isolated from, and unconcerned with, the experiences of discrimination such as busing that affect different racial groups. However, since coming to college, she came to recognize that "you really have to work to put yourself in the other's situation or to understand something outside of where you come from . . . because it takes a lot for you to understand that life might be different. . . . I think I try to understand what life is like for other people. I think I'm pretty concerned with everyone having equal opportunity."

Like Ana and Rose, in her senior-year interview Leslie suggested that all three social identities were related; however, she still struggled to articulate the interconnections among them, suggesting that while college provides many opportunities for identity development, emerging adults have not yet completed their identity projects. Often it was in their narratives about their daily life experiences, not in their discussions about their current and future career pathways, that participants articulated most clearly and spontaneously the intersections between their personal and social identities.

Conclusion

In sum, although we found a general pattern of increasing integration and sophistication in how emerging adults understand and speak about their career, ethnicity, gender, and social class identities, there was great variability in the timing, sequence, and degree of understanding that they showed. This variability is due in part to the vast array of experiences that influence their identity development, the salience and centrality of their various identities, and the strategies and other psychological work that they use to make meaning of these experiences. The emerging adult participants also varied in their articulation of connections among their multiple identities and whether the intersection of personal and social identities was tied to specific experiences or placed in the broader context of society.

Clearly emerging adulthood is a developmental period characterized by continued identity negotiations. Indeed, we agree with Erikson's original conceptualizations of identity as a lifelong developmental project. As illustrated by the six chapters that follow, this identity project begins in childhood, and although emerging adults often have made much headway in their personal and social identity constructions, their identity projects are far from complete and will likely be revisited as they move through the new roles, relationships, and developmental periods of their lives.

References

Arnett, J. J. (2004). *Emerging adulthood: The winding road from the late teens through the twenties*. New York: Oxford University Press.

Ashmore, R. D., Deaux, K., & McLaughlin-Volpe, T. (2004). An organizing framework for collective identity: Articulation and significance of multidimensionality. *Psychological Bulletin, 130*(1), 80–114.

Bourdieu, P. (1977). *Outline of a theory of practice*. Cambridge: Cambridge University Press.

Coleman, J. (1988). Social capital in the creation of human capital. *American Journal of Sociology, 94*(suppl.), 95–120.

Cooper, C. R. (1999). Multiple selves, multiple worlds: Cultural perspectives on individuality and connectedness in adolescent development. In A. Masten (Ed.), *Minnesota symposia on child psychology: Culture and development* (pp. 25–57). Mahwah, NJ: Erlbaum.

Cooper, C. R., Behrens, R., & Trinh, N. (in press). Identity development. In R. A. Shweder, T. R. Bidell, A. C. Dailey, S. D. Dixon, P. J. Miller, & J. Model (Eds.), *The Chicago companion to the child*. Chicago: University of Chicago Press.

Cooper, C. R., Cooper, R. G., Azmitia, M., Chavira, G., & Gullat, Y. (2002). Bridging multiple worlds: How African American and Latino youth in academic outreach programs navigate math pathways to college. *Applied Developmental Science, 6*, 73–87.

Cross, W. E. Jr. (1995). In search of Blackness and Afrocentricity: The psychology of Black identity change. In H. W. Harris, H. C. Blue, & E.E.H. Griffith (Eds.), *Racial and ethnic identity: Psychological development and creative expression* (pp. 53–72). Florence, KY: Taylor & Frances/Routledge.

Deaux, K., & Perkins, T. S. (2001). The kaleidoscopic self. In C. Sedikides & M. B. Brewer (Eds.), *Individual self, relational self, collective self* (pp. 299–313). Philadelphia: Psychology Press.

Dixson, A. D., & Rousseau, C. K. (2005). And we are still not saved: Critical race theory in education 10 years later. In A. D. Dixson & C. K. Rousseau (Eds.), *Critical race theory in education* (pp. 31–56). New York: Routledge.

Erikson, E. E. (1968). *Identity: Youth and crisis.* New York: Norton.

Fuligni, A. J., & Flook, L. (2005). A social identity approach to ethnic differences in family relationships during adolescence. In R. Kail (Ed.), *Advances in child development and behavior, 33* (pp. 125–152). Orlando, FL: Academic Press.

Harding, S. (Ed.). (2004). *The feminist standpoint reader.* New York: Routledge.

Harter, S. (1999). *The construction of the self. A developmental perspective.* New York: Guilford Press.

hooks, b. (2003). Reflections on race and sex. In A. Darder, M. Baltodano, & R. D. Torres (Eds.), *The critical pedagogy reader* (pp. 238–244). New York: Routledge.

Marcia, J. (1980). Identity in adolescence. In J. Adelson (Ed.), *Handbook of adolescent psychology* (pp. 159–197). Hoboken, NJ: Wiley.

McAdams, D. P. (2001). The psychology of life stories. *Review of General Psychology, 5,* 100–122.

Penuel, W. R., & Wertsch, J. V. (1995). Vygotsky and identity formation: A sociocultural approach. *Educational Psychologist, 30,* 83–92.

Phinney, J. S. (1990). Ethnic identity in adolescents and adults: A review of research. *Psychological Bulletin, 108,* 499–514.

Phinney, J. S. (2003). Ethnic identity and acculturation. In K. M. Chun, P. Balls-Organista, & G. Marín (Eds.), *Acculturation: Advances in theory, measurement, and applied research* (pp. 63–81). Washington, DC: American Psychological Association.

Quintana, S. M. (2007). Racial and ethnic identity: Developmental perspectives and research. *Journal of Counseling Psychology, 54,* 259–270.

Ruble, D., Alvarez, J., Bachman, M., Cameron, J., Fuligni, A., & Garcia Coll, C. (2004). The development of a sense of "we": The emergence and implications of children's collective identity. In M. Bennett & F. Sani (Eds.), *The development of the social self* (pp. 29–76). New York: Psychology Press.

Syed, M., & Azmitia, M. (in press). A narrative approach to ethnic identity in emerging adulthood: Bringing life to the identity status model. *Developmental Psychology.*

Tajfel, H. (1981). *Human groups and social categories: Studies in social psychology.* Cambridge: Cambridge University Press.

Tajfel, H., & Turner, J. C. (1986). The social identity theory of intergroup behavior. In S. Worchel & W. Austin (Eds.), *Psychology of intergroup relations* (pp. 7–24). Chicago: Nelson-Hall.

Thorne, A. (2004). Putting the person into social identity. *Human Development, 47,* 361–365.

Waters, M. C. (1996). The intersection of gender, race, and ethnicity in identity development of Caribbean American teens. In B.J.R. Leadbeater & N. Way (Eds.), *Urban girls: Resisting stereotypes, creating identities* (pp. 65–84). New York: New York University Press.

MARGARITA AZMITIA *is a professor of developmental psychology at the University of California at Santa Cruz.*

MOIN SYED *is a doctoral student at the University of California at Santa Cruz.*

KIMBERLY RADMACHER *is an assistant professor of human development at the California State University, Dominguez Hills.*

NEW DIRECTIONS FOR CHILD AND ADOLESCENT DEVELOPMENT • DOI: 10.1002/cd

Hurtado, A., & Silva, J. M. (2008). Creating new social identities in children through critical multicultural media: The case of *Little Bill*. In M. Azmitia, M. Syed, & K. Radmacher
(Eds.), *The intersections of personal and social identities. New Directions for Child and Adolescent Development, 120,* 17–30.

2

Creating New Social Identities in Children Through Critical Multicultural Media: The Case of *Little Bill*

Aída Hurtado, Janelle M. Silva

Abstract

*Multicultural education emerged from the political struggles of the 1960s and
1970s and advocated the inclusion of women and ethnic and racial groups in
school curricula and children's media. Recently multiculturalism has evolved to
include a critical perspective by focusing on stigmatized social identities such
as race, class, sexuality, ethnicity, and disability. Little Bill, a children's animated
television series, is an example of applied critical multiculturalism. In this chapter, we present a case study of one episode, "A Ramp for Monty," to illustrate the
merits of this approach, which may increase the number of social identities children relate to and increase the degree of understanding they may bring to the
differences inherent in social identities.* © Wiley Periodicals, Inc.

NEW DIRECTIONS FOR CHILD AND ADOLESCENT DEVELOPMENT, no. 120, Summer 2008 © Wiley Periodicals, Inc.
Published online in Wiley InterScience (www.interscience.wiley.com) • DOI: 10.1002/cd.213

Childhood in the United States is historically conceptualized as the stage in life requiring protection from life's harsh realities, including the consequences of such social inequalities as poverty, racism, sexism, homophobia, and classism (among other unpleasant social realities). This unquestioned assumption was challenged in the 1970s as the civil rights movements brought social injustices to the forefront and advocated radical change in all institutions, including childhood, to address social inequalities. Positive consequences of such mobilization were the acknowledgment that people of color have been treated unequally in society and that these inequalities begin in childhood. Innovative social programs such as Head Start were implemented as part of the U.S. government's War on Poverty.

The civil rights movements and social upheavals of the 1960s and 1970s also led to a critical examination of schooling in the United States; curricula, teaching practices, and media were an integral part of this reassessment (Banks, 1995). These societal forces gave rise to what became known as multicultural education, most recently referred to within educational circles as the diversity movement. However, opening the curricula to include multiple cultural and racial groups and to examine gender relations critically did not necessarily abandon the notion of a protected childhood. Rather, multiculturalism reinscribed the image of childhood in our society with a new metaphor; society was conceived as a "salad" composed of many different kinds of "vegetables," or children, all of equal value and contributing equally to the final dish. The difficult issues of children growing up in inner cities, exposed to violence, lacking adequate health care, living in poverty, and so on were not deemed appropriate subject matter for a multicultural curriculum or children's media. By adopting the multicultural metaphor of the bountiful salad, the harsh realities of life remained unexposed and the revered concept of innocent childhood remained intact.

Critical Consciousness as "Spontaneous Combustion"

Although creating a protected space for childhood may seem a desirable objective for society, it does not facilitate the socialization of a critical consciousness in children facing social inequalities. Even adolescence is typically conceptualized as a protected developmental phase in which exposure to complicated and contradictory views on political and social inequalities is largely restricted or deemed not comprehensible cognitively. In too many instances, the first time youth encounter the invisible histories of ethnic and racial groups, gender inequality and its machinations in society, and the nature of economic deprivation is when they enter institutions of higher education. In many ways, a university education can be a jarring experience, a rude awakening. It is only then, as young adults, that they are deemed cognitively ready to be instructed from a critical and complicated perspective that may lead to political consciousness.

NEW DIRECTIONS FOR CHILD AND ADOLESCENT DEVELOPMENT • DOI: 10.1002/cd

Ideally the development of a critical social consciousness should not happen through "spontaneous combustion." An extensive process of examination, or even reeducation, of what is commonly held to be true and valid in society is required to understand that certain social conditions should not be the basis for negative evaluation. The multicultural education movement in the 1970s advocated the restructuring of educational materials and pedagogy to awaken ethnic, racial, and gender awareness in children at an earlier age than accepted by the notion of a protected childhood. However, as earnest as the multicultural education movement was in its motivation, its implementation, especially in children's television, usually gave way to the salad approach. In essence, social inequalities were suspended in the protected, make-believe worlds of children's cartoons and educational programming. Fortunately, there were exceptions in television. Programs like *Sesame Street* introduced impressive innovations; unlike previous children's programming in which diversity of any kind was rarely, if ever, seen, *Sesame Street* included children of different ethnic and racial groups and gender, portraying them positively and encouraging open-mindedness and egalitarian attitudes.

Critical Multiculturalism as Embodied in Intersectionality

Multicultural education was a critical intervention, highlighting previously ignored ethnic and racial groups in the United States. But researchers and practitioners alike gradually recognized that by ignoring the origins and processes of group oppressions, multiculturalism in education was being homogenized. Poignant social issues born of differences in social, political, and economic power were nonexistent in multicultural curricula and certainly not present in children's multicultural television. This missing element in multiculturalism created an aperture: a critical dimension to this movement in education was needed to fill the void.

Several dimensions of racial and ethnic culture were essential to making multicultural education critical. One of these was the introduction of the painful aspects of group histories. For example, critical multiculturalism advocates that school curricula include historical topics such as slavery in the United States, the internment of Japanese Americans during World War II, and the U.S. colonization of the Southwest. These histories are all critical moments in this country's past and are essential to the definition of self among individuals with these ethnic and racial histories. An explicit antiracist agenda is also considered bedrock to a critical multicultural education. A central concern is that ethnic and racial cultures not be essentialized to stereotypes echoed in media portrayals. Essentialism can be avoided by emphasizing the diversity within groups—their many histories, immigration patterns, languages (English as well as native languages), class differences, and geographical locations within the United States (for example, Chicanas in Texas versus Cuban Americans in Miami). In essence, a critical

NEW DIRECTIONS FOR CHILD AND ADOLESCENT DEVELOPMENT • DOI: 10.1002/cd

multiculturalism emphasizes hybridity and variation rather than consistency and homogenization.

From a social psychological perspective, critical multiculturalism is embodied in individuals' social identities. Social identities—race, class, ethnicity, and so on—are explicitly defined within social psychological theory, as proposed by Henri Tajfel (1981) and his followers, and have predictable consequences for social and individual behavior. Feminist scholars of color have expanded critical multiculturalism by including those identities used to subordinate women. To appreciate the process and impact of social identities, we turn to their definition and implications for intersectionality.

The Creation of Social Identities

Several theoretical distinctions elucidate the processes that individuals undergo in constructing their social identities. The foremost distinction held by most social psychologists is between personal and social identity, which together form a person's total sense of self. Tajfel (1981) posits that personal identity is that aspect of self composed of psychological traits and dispositions that give rise to personal uniqueness. Personal identity is derived from intrapsychic influences, many of which are socialized within families (however they are defined). From this perspective, human beings have a great deal in common precisely because their personal identities comprise universal processes such as loving, mating, and doing productive work—activities that are considered universal components of self. However, these universal components of self are filtered through language, culture, historical moment, and social structures. For example, children in all societies are considered to belong to their biological parents, not to neighbors, aunts, uncles, or other relatives. However, there are infinite variations in the constellations considered appropriate for raising children—from an entire village, to a nuclear family, to foster care.

Tajfel considers personal identities, which are not as socially salient as social identities, to be much more stable and coherent over time than social identities. An individual's gender, race, ethnicity, and socioeconomic class are relevant in most social contexts. As such, the presentation of self is regulated through these group memberships in most social interactions such that coherence is a necessary prerequisite for social functioning. For example, an individual categorized as a man cannot dress as a woman one day and a man the next without social (and sometimes violent) consequences. According to Tajfel, personal identity is for the most part a private sense of "me-ness" (see Chapter One, this volume) that is not necessarily negotiated or challenged in every social interaction. For instance, people generally consider themselves kind and open-minded; until someone or some incident challenges them on this self-assessment, there is no reason to doubt their judgment. In the ordinary course of social events, the unchallenged personal self-assessment lacks motivation for reevaluation of the personal self. Although not universally accepted among developmental psychologists,

Tajfel's theory of self addresses intergroup relations, not intrapsychic influences that may lead to changes in personal identity. How and under what circumstances changes in social identity may lead to changes (or not) in personal identity is yet to be theoretically explored and empirically determined.

In contrast, social identity is that aspect of self derived from the knowledge of being part of social categories and groups, together with the value and emotional significance attached to those group formations. Tajfel argues that the creation of social identities is the consequence of three social psychological processes. The first is social categorization. Nationality, language, race and ethnicity, skin color, and other social or physical characteristics that are meaningful in particular social contexts can be the basis for social categorization and thus the foundation for the creation of social identities. Although Tajfel based social identity theory on adults, the theory has also been applied to children's development of social identities (Bigler, Jones, & Lobliner, 1997; Chapter Three, this volume). Children seem to be able to categorize social identities that are perceptually salient, such as gender and race, earlier than social identities that are based on more complex markers like ethnicity (Bernal, Knight, Garza, Ocampo, & Cota, 1990). In terms of social class, Ramsey (1991) finds that although four-and-half-year-old children can make dichotomous judgments between "rich" and "poor" people portrayed in photographs, they are "unable to explain where money comes from" (p. 80). In fact, when asked what "rich" means, "some of the children used words such as 'gold' and 'kings,' which reflect the fairy tale images of wealth that appear in many books and movies for children" (p. 79). It is not until children are older that they begin to comprehend social class beyond "rudimentary understanding of how the economy works" (p. 81).

Another process underlying the construction of social identities is social comparison. In this process, a group's status, degree of affluence, or other characteristic achieves significance in relation to perceived differences and their value connotations from other social formations. For example, many Latina university students mention that as children, they were not completely aware of their poverty because everyone around them had the same economic status. It was not until they reached adulthood and left their impoverished communities for affluent university environments that they fully grasped the nature of class differences (Hurtado, 2003).

The third process involves psychological work, both cognitive and emotional, that is prompted by what Tajfel claims is a universal motive: the achievement of a positive sense of self. The social groups and social identities that present the greatest obstacles to a positive sense of self are those that are disparaged (including "invisible" identities, such as sexual orientation), those that have to be negotiated frequently because of their visibility (physical attributes, for example, such as dark skin color), those that have become politicized by social movements, and so on. Moreover, these social identities become especially powerful psychologically; they are easily accessible and dwelled on, likely to be salient across situations, and likely to function as schemata, frameworks, or social scripts (Hurtado & Gurin, 2004). For example, a poor, gay, African American adolescent with a physical disability is more likely to reflect heavily on his social identities than is a middle-class, White, heterosexual adolescent with no physical impediments. Unproblematic group memberships—ones that are socially valued, accorded privilege, or invisible to others—may not even become social identities. For instance, until very recently, being White and male was not the subject of inquiry and is still not widely thought of as a social identity (Hurtado & Stewart, 2004). In addition, having a characteristic that could potentially become a social identity, such as being female, does not necessarily mean that the individual develops such a social identity; some consciousness of what that particular category signifies socially is necessary for identity constructions.

Because individuals belong to multiple groups determined by race, gender, and other attributes, they construct multiple social identities. Social identities gain particular significance when they represent "master statuses." Race, social class, gender, ethnicity, physical disabilities, and sexuality are the social identities assigned master statuses because individuals must psychologically negotiate their potentially stigmatizing effects. In the United States, as in many other countries, master statuses are used to make value judgments about group memberships. Tajfel's theory of social identity provides a sophisticated framework for understanding how individuals make sense of their group memberships—both unproblematic and stigmatized ones.

Thus, social identity, consisting of an individual's group affiliations and emotional attachments to those group memberships, is largely derived from social comparisons made as individuals mature and position themselves within larger society. The meaning of an individual's group affiliation—its value and significance—is based on the presence and significance of other social formations in the environment. When positive or negative values are attached to group affiliations, individuals have to do psychological work to come to terms with their social identities, using cognitive skills that vary by developmental age. As Tajfel posits, individuals strive not only to be socially different from other groups, the difference has to be positive.

Intersectionality in Social Identity Theory

The concept of intersectionality was shaped by feminist scholars and has facilitated an understanding of the social and economic conditions of women of color, traditionally considered problematic social categories (Hurtado, 2003; Sandoval, 2000). Sociologist Patricia Hill Collins (2000) broadly describes several components of intersectionality:

> The very notion of the intersections of race, class, and gender as an area worthy of study emerged from the recognition of practitioners of each distinctive theoretical tradition that inequality could not be explained, let alone chal-

lenged, via a race-only, or gender-only framework. No one had all of the answers and no one was going to get all of the answers without attention to two things. First, the notion of interlocking oppressions refers to the macro-level connections linking systems of oppression such as race, class, and gender. This is a model describing the social structures that create social positions. Second, the notion of intersectionality describes micro-level processes—namely, how each individual and group occupies a social position within interlocking structures of oppression described by the metaphor of intersectionality. Together they shape oppression [p. 82].

Intersectionality theorists argue that gender-only or race-only analyses do not lead to an understanding of the position of all women or to a dismantling of the structures that oppress them. Notably these scholars also refuse to rank oppressions, say, by order of significance or degree of stigmatization; instead, they argue, it is membership in oppressed social formations (such as being poor, of color, or lesbian) and their pattern of intersection that determine women's experiences of oppression.

The intersectionality framework has had an enormous influence in many academic fields, including political science, sociology, psychology, and the humanities. Hurtado (2003) links Tajfel's theory of social identity to the theoretical framework of intersectionality, contending that from a social psychological point of view, intersectionality refers to the particular constellation of social identities that are the primary basis for stigmatization: class, race, sexuality, gender, ethnicity, and physical ableness. Stigmatized social identities intersect and form alternating constellations in various social spaces. Consequently, the significance and relationship between these social identities (such as class, race, ethnicity, and sexuality) vary from social sphere to social sphere and across time. In some circumstances, one particular group membership or set of memberships may be more important than others; for example, when functioning within a group that is homogeneous with regard to their significant social identities, that particular social identity (or identities) may be much less relevant than it would be in a situation where many groups interact with each other. A high school student may not think about being Mexican when interacting with family members, for example, but may be acutely aware of this identity when answering a question in a classroom where he or she is the only person of Mexican descent. In addition, a person may define a particular group membership differently at one time than at another. For example, a young person growing up in a predominantly Chicano/a neighborhood may take his or her ethnicity for granted. Attending a university and taking courses on Chicano history and culture may provide the impetus for this person to reassess ethnicity and its salience and importance (Hurtado & Gurin, 2004). A social identity framework allows the examination of this complexity in various social spheres, in different life cycles, and across historical moments.

Implementing Critical Multiculturalism in Children's Television: A Case Study

What might an age-appropriate media project espousing a critical multicultural perspective look like? How can leading ideas be introduced into children's media to affect consciousness and begin to cement the repertoire necessary for recognizing stigmatized social identities and questioning unearned privileges? We present a critical analysis of an episode from the television series *Little Bill*. This case study was drawn from a recent more comprehensive research project based on the entire series.

Little Bill. The *Little Bill* series, which premiered in 1999, is the brainchild of actor-writer Bill Cosby. The main character, Little Bill, is a five-year-old African American boy who lives with his parents; older sister, April; older brother, Bobby; and great-grandmother, Alice the Great. *Little Bill* is a particularly noteworthy example of applied critical multiculturalism: in our broader study of ten randomly selected episodes (two vignettes per episode), we found that each story addresses a different stigmatized identity (or set of identities), constituting the concept of intersectionality and, as we are proposing, the principles of critical multiculturalism.

The treatment of *Little Bill* broadens the application of critical multiculturalism beyond the media's prior boundaries. Through an artful use of narrative and animation, the show systematically debunks many of the negative facets of the social identities ascribed to people of color in general and to African Americans in particular. The episodes are not designed to preach a message or convey a lesson. Rather, the story communicates the value and implications of derogated social identities and reinscribes these identities with new content and meaning. In a single episode of the series, "A Ramp for Monty," no fewer than four racialization processes (in order of appearance, intellectual competence, phenotypes, parenting, and gender roles), all having direct consequence on social identities, are reevaluated. The theoretical paradigm of intersectionality facilitates the simultaneous examination of these multiple social identities intersecting in various social contexts. The *Little Bill* series captures the social reality essential to understanding oppression and stigma: individuals are presented in their everyday lives experiencing their social identities as fluid and overlapping, not as one social identity at a time. The context and the social relations largely determine which social identity becomes salient.

As implied in the title "A Ramp for Monty," the foremost intervention in this *Little Bill* episode is to rethink how an able child should relate to a physically disabled one. Should the disability be ignored? Should it be considered a handicap for which the able child feels sorry, reinforcing a paternalistic perspective toward those less fortunate? Should the physically disabled child be first subject to teasing and later accepted, elevating the able child's moral transformation to the central theme and relegating the physically challenged child to the background? Consider, instead, the storyline that takes critical multiculturalism seriously: initially no distinction

NEW DIRECTIONS FOR CHILD AND ADOLESCENT DEVELOPMENT • DOI: 10.1002/cd

between the children is shown because it is not relevant until a physical hurdle is introduced, at which point the able child takes equal responsibility for making his friend comfortable, thus demonstrating the true meaning of friendship. "A Ramp for Monty" takes the latter approach while addressing the central theme (and social identity) of the physically disabled. This episode of *Little Bill* simultaneously presents other stigmatized social identities, subtly reinscribing them as it works toward a resolution to the central plot.

The Social Context of *Little Bill*. *Little Bill*'s core mission is to communicate that African American communities are not violent, chaotic places full of dysfunction, populated by people who only speak Black English and dress like gangster rappers. The series also highlights the importance and diversity of African American culture, history, and social relations, going beyond the stereotypes usually shown in children's media. The world that Little Bill lives in is peaceful, filled with love and gentleness. Although Little Bill lives with both of his parents, the family extends beyond the nuclear model, including a great-grandmother whose presence completes a trigenerational household. The *Little Bill* episodes portray this alternative community within, not distinct from, the urban communities depicted in other media. The opening scene in "A Ramp for Monty" is of the Philadelphia skyline, although the landscape might be found in any other major U.S. city: Chicago, New York, Detroit, Boston, all urban centers with sizable African American populations. The selection of an urban setting is significant, informing us that peaceful, loving families can and do exist in cities too.

Restituting Derogated Social Identities. The first time Little Bill and Monty are introduced in "A Ramp for Monty," they are sitting together in the library, an unusual choice of settings for African American boys in a television program. After all, African Americans are supposed to be anti-intellectual and antiacademic. The two boys are not playing basketball or hanging out on a street corner with their "homies": instead they are in a library exploring and enjoying books. They giggle as someone passes, and Little Bill reminds Monty to quiet down because they are in a library. They know to be respectful of this place of learning. Their demeanor and joy convey that they belong in a library, that they are not intruders disrupting a space alien to them. Little Bill shares a book on dinosaurs with Monty, pointing out characteristics, like a long neck, that allowed the dinosaurs to reach leaves in tall trees. The activity the boys engage in is further evidence that they enjoy learning. The boys' playfulness and comfort with acquiring knowledge help to reinscribe the learning space of the library as a habitat familiar, not alien, to African American children.

Next, a librarian, who is a fair-skinned African American, approaches the boys. Although she has red hair and freckles, she otherwise appears to be African American. The librarian's speech style, while highly educated, has an African American cadence. Her fair-skinned phenotype visually suggests the diversity within African American communities. This unexpected depiction of an African American woman is typical throughout the episode.

NEW DIRECTIONS FOR CHILD AND ADOLESCENT DEVELOPMENT • DOI: 10.1002/cd

For example, Little Bill's mother has very dark skin, his father is lighter, and his own skin color lies somewhere between both parents. Also, all of the characters in the series have facial features that are decidedly distinct from one another, instead of the characteristic bulging eyes, broad nose, and full lips of the stereotype. Through its visual emphasis on diversity, the series informs young viewers (as well as adults) about the variety of phenotypes in African American communities (and, by extension, other communities of color).

After a playful yet educational exchange with the librarian, Little Bill and Monty look for Little Bill's father, whom they find reading a newspaper in another section of the library. There are several significant dimensions in the representation of the father. Instead of portraying Little Bill's mother as the caretaker, his father is shown to be in charge of the two young boys. His presence in the library refutes the notion that in the rare instances when African American boys are interested in knowledge, it is independent of parental influence. In this case, the father is found reading, an indicator of his direct influence on his son's academic interests, similar to an influence more often associated with white middle-class parents. Notably, Little Bill is not an outlier in his community; Monty is equally invested in learning; both boys are deeply immersed in the world of dinosaurs. Later in the episode, we learn that Monty's grandmother is raising him, reinforcing the conviction that intellectual behavior can be socialized in nontraditional families, including those headed by women.

As the father and boys leave the library, Monty's difference is addressed for the first time. When they approach the exit, it becomes obvious that Monty cannot use the stairs because of his wheelchair. However, the chair, instead of being an obstacle, becomes an asset as Monty with outstretched arms soars down the ramp, pretending to fly like the dinosaurs. Little Bill follows closely behind. The occasion is used to highlight the children's imagination and mutual intellectual engagement rather than to emphasize Monty's physical disability. The joyous scene subverts the gloominess of acknowledging stigma. By approaching difference as natural or even as an asset, the scene demonstrates resistance to stigma (as it is called in the feminist literature) or resilience (from the psychological literature).

As the episode progresses, Little Bill's parents further exemplify an egalitarian family through their actions. In addition to caretaking, Little Bill's father prepares meals for the family and helps with "women's chores" in the home. The story now turns to Little Bill's realization that Monty's wheelchair restricts him from playing in the backyard. Little Bill is silently pondering this insight as he and his father wash the dinner dishes. Noticing Little Bill's consternation, his father inquires about what is on his mind, another instance of atypical gender behavior as the father notices emotion and explores rather than ignores it. Little Bill is distressed that Monty cannot enter the backyard without the assistance of his father. This scene illustrates the psychological work, as proposed by Tajfel, called "triggers" or "encounters" by others (see Chapter One, this volume), that is necessary for Little Bill to undertake in order to deal with the unequal treatment his friend Monty experiences because of his difference. Little Bill is engaging in social comparison between his status as an able child and Monty's as a disabled one. He is also becoming aware that the social comparison is not neutral as Monty experiences restrictions he does not. Monty's categorization based on his limited mobility results in stigma because society has not invested resources to make all spaces accessible to people like Monty. Little Bill's response to the existing situation represents what Tajfel calls cognitive alternatives. Instead of changing the individual, the person using cognitive alternatives perceives ways of changing the context to reduce group stigma.

In this case, Little Bill asks his father whether they can build a ramp like the one in the library so Monty can join him in the yard. In the next few scenes, Little Bill and his father jointly build the ramp, conversing as they work. There are no women present in these scenes to do the emotional work of bridging father and son, nor is their discussion a gender-based banter highlighting masculinity. Rather, the conversation between father and son is joyful, playful, informative, kind, and caring. There is never mention of stigma or disadvantage when discussing the ramp. The ramp is presented as a natural adjustment to a hurdle, with no teachable moment in which the authority figure explains to the child why he should be kind to someone who is less "advantaged" than him.

In the final scene, Monty's grandmother drops her grandson off at Little Bill's home to play. Little Bill surprises Monty with the ramp and suggests, "Let's go play dinosaurs outside!" Monty replies, "No, I want to play flying Montysaurus," as he raises his arms and races down the ramp built by Little Bill and his father.

Discussion

According to Henry A. Giroux (2003), critical multiculturalism examines how "power [is] designed to exclude, contain or disadvantage the oppressed" (p. 88). Critical multiculturalism advocates the use of formal and informal education, including media, to teach students about oppression, domination, and power relations in society. In promoting critical multiculturalism, parents are essentially being asked to help increase the number of social identities their children are exposed to during important periods of their development, not an easy task. In children's television, it is almost entirely unprecedented to portray children with a critical consciousness about oppression based on belonging to stigmatized social formations. Previous multicultural education had as its delicate task the exposure of attitudes toward stigmatized groups without the subjection of children to the unpleasantries of racism, sexism, classism, homophobia, poverty, and other social inequalities. Critical multicultural theorists, as well as feminist writers of color, have pushed the parameters further by advocating that children not delay gaining a political consciousness until young adulthood. By that developmental stage, social identities and stigmatization have already been fixed by dominant hegemonic explanations that reaffirm the status quo. Instead, children should be socialized to the inequalities embodied in social identities early on. The *Little Bill* series is one of the few children's programs that have taken on this challenge.

The contour that makes *Little Bill* a successful multicultural program is the series' commitment to weave a critical perspective on stigmatized social identities through the narrative. By examining the processes of racialization, genderization, and ethnicization as critically portrayed in *Little Bill,* our study contributes to the burgeoning literature on the development of children's social identities (Bigler et al., 1997; see Chapter Three, this volume). The critical perspective of *Little Bill* is particularly effective because it never explicitly states its goal of reevaluating stigmatized social identities, thus avoiding an overbearing, self-righteous tone. Instead, the overarching mechanism of critical portrayal is simply a humane and loving world in which individuals treat each other as individuals; at the same time, the real differences, as represented through individuals' social identities, are not elided or distorted to fit a nonexistent perfect world. The positive aspects of language (Black expression, for example, or phrases and words from other cultures such as Yiddish) are highlighted, as is the possibility of friendships across differences, including age, gender, ethnicity, and race.

The fact that Monty is in a wheelchair is not a hindrance to the friendship between the boys. The episode instead highlights the joy the boys experience from exploring books, the imagination they display when they play "dinosaurs," and the love and affirmation they receive from the adults: Little Bill's parents, the librarian, and Monty's grandmother. The subject of Monty's physical limitation is used to illustrate how it can be overcome with sensitivity and in the natural course of being a good friend. Monty's condition is not objectified to illustrate the central character's importance, heightened consciousness, or paternalistic caring toward someone "less fortunate" than himself. Monty is Little Bill's friend and as such is treated with dignity and respect.

Future Directions for Research

The goal in studying social identities from a Tajfelian framework is to illustrate the arbitrary and socially constructed nature of stigma. Furthermore, stigmatization is not random but largely dependent on intergroup dynamics where more powerful groups stigmatize less powerful ones to naturalize the uneven distributions of power and resources. Within this framework, the stigma often attributed to social categories is not objectively real but socially constructed. Intersectional feminist scholarship is also aimed at deconstructing the arbitrary nature of oppression based on social categorization. As such, The *Little Bill* series is aimed at diminishing out-group and in-group comparisons to destigmatize socially constructed categories by demonstrating the positive aspects of belonging to such categories. Both goals are consistent with social identity theory because at its core, it is not social categorization that is detrimental to social existence but rather the assignment of stigma to enforce and justify unequal treatment of particular social formations. To date, there has not been an assessment of whether the *Little Bill* series accomplishes its goal of diminishing stigma for various social identities and replacing it with positive views of self for its young audiences. We are in the process of designing a series of experiments with children to assess the benefits, if any, of the *Little Bill* series on children's social and personal identities. Future research will have to address how parents and other socializing agents, like siblings and teachers, can play a role in conjunction with television programming in increasing children's awareness and reevaluation of stigmatized social identities.

Without a doubt, the *Little Bill* series embodies not only a critical multiculturalism but also a theoretical concept of intersectionality, as proposed by feminist scholars of color. However, there are still aspects of intersectionality that *Little Bill* does not address; for example, in the randomly selected ten episodes analyzed in our comprehensive study, there is no mention of gay or lesbian families. As a series, the objective of *Little Bill* is to demonstrate the diversity in African American communities by portraying the loving families and communal relationships that exist alongside more troubled African American existences in this country. However, there is not a single direct mention of poverty or violence in any of the episodes. The next frontier in children's television programming in general and in *Little Bill* specifically is to fully address all of the social identities that stigmatize individuals and communities so that the world so lovingly portrayed in *Little Bill* is indeed a total reality.

References

Banks, J. A. (1995). Multicultural education: Historical development, dimensions, and practice. In J. A. Banks & C. A. McGee Banks (Eds.), *Handbook of research on multicultural education* (pp. 3–24). New York: Macmillan.

Bernal, M. E., Knight, G. P., Garza, C. A., Ocampo, K. A., & Cota, M. (1990). The development of ethnic identity in Mexican-American children. *Hispanic Journal of Behavioral Sciences, 12*(1), 3–24.

Bigler, R. S., Jones, L. C., & Lobliner, D. B. (1997). Social categorization and the formation of intergroup attitudes in children. *Child Development, 68*(3), 530–543.

Collins, P. H. (2000). *Black feminist thought.* New York: Routledge.

Giroux, H. A. (2003). Pedagogies of difference, race, and representation: Film as a site of translation and politics. In P. P. Tirfonas (Ed.), *Pedagogies of difference: Rethinking education for social change* (pp. 83–109). New York: Routledge Falmer.

Hurtado, A. (2003). *Voicing Chicana feminisms: Young women speak out on sexuality and identity.* New York: New York University Press.

Hurtado, A., & Gurin, P. (2004). ¿Quién soy? ¿Quienes somos? (Who am I? Who are we?): Chicana/o identity in a changing U.S. society. Tucson: University of Arizona Press.

Hurtado, A., & Stewart, A. J. (2004). Through the looking glass: Implications of studying whiteness for feminist methods. In M. Fine, L. Weis, L. Powell Pruitt, & A. Burns

(Eds.), *Off white: Readings on power, privilege, and resistance* (pp. 315–330). New York: Routledge.

Ramsey, P. G. (1991). Young children's awareness and understanding of social class differences. *Journal of Genetic Psychology, 152*(1), 71–82.

Sandoval, C. (2000). *Methodology of the oppressed.* Minneapolis: University of Minnesota Press.

Tajfel, H. (1981). *Human groups and social categories: Studies in social psychology.* Cambridge: Cambridge University Press.

AÍDA HURTADO is a professor of psychology and director of the Chicano/Latino Research Center at the University of California at Santa Cruz.

JANELLE M. SILVA is a doctoral student in psychology at the University of California at Santa Cruz

NEW DIRECTIONS FOR CHILD AND ADOLESCENT DEVELOPMENT • DOI: 10.1002/cd

Lurye, L. E., Zosuls, K. M., & Ruble, D. N. (2008). Gender identity and adjustment: Understanding the impact of individual and normative differences in sex typing. In M. Azmitia, M. Syed, & K. Radmacher (Eds.), *The intersections of personal and social identities.*
New Directions for Child and Adolescent Development, 120, 31–46.

3

Gender Identity and Adjustment: Understanding the Impact of Individual and Normative Differences in Sex Typing

Leah E. Lurye, Kristina M. Zosuls, Diane N. Ruble

Abstract

The relationship among gender identity, sex typing, and adjustment has attracted the attention of social and developmental psychologists for many years. However, they have explored this issue with different assumptions and different approaches. Generally the approaches differ regarding whether sex typing is considered adaptive versus maladaptive, measured as an individual or normative difference, and whether gender identity is regarded as a unidimensional or multidimensional construct. In this chapter, we consider both perspectives and suggest that the developmental timing and degree of sex typing, as well as the multidimensionality of gender identity, be considered when examining their relationship to adjustment. © Wiley Periodicals, Inc.

This research was supported in part by a grant from the National Institutes of Health
(5RO1HD049994) awarded to Diane N. Ruble.

W hether it is based on sex, skin color, or even determined arbitrarily, membership in a social group exerts a profound influence on human behavior, with both positive and negative implications. Specifically membership in a social group has been shown to promote a positive social identity from which individuals can derive self-esteem and a sense of belongingness or connectedness to others and serve as a buffer during times of stress. However, membership in a social group can also promote negative biases toward out-group members, derogation of in-group members who violate group norms, and disengagement from certain areas in which one's group has been negatively stereotyped (for example, women and math).

Given its obvious implications for psychological well-being, it is not surprising that the study of social group membership has attracted the attention of psychologists. Both social and developmental psychologists have studied the effects of intergroup bias on individuals' behaviors and self-evaluations, the extent to which identification with a stigmatized group affects well-being, and the influence of group membership on personal choices and behaviors (see Ruble et al., 2004, for a review). Although psychologists have studied a wide range of social group memberships, the documented consequences of belonging to a gender group are among the most studied and most controversial. Within the domain of gender, psychologists have devoted considerable attention to the relationship between gender and well-being, and one issue in particular—the relationship between adherence to gender norms and adjustment—has elicited different assumptions and different approaches among social and developmental psychologists. Broadly, the divergence in perspectives can be characterized in terms of whether sex typing is considered adaptive or maladaptive, described as an individual or normative difference, and whether gender identity is regarded as a unidimensional or multidimensional construct.

In this chapter, we address the three themes of this volume: interdisciplinarity in the study of identity development, developmental processes, and the intersection between personal and social identities. To address each theme, we review perspectives on the relationship between sex typing and adjustment. Specifically, we consider past conclusions that sex typing may be adaptive or maladaptive.

In terms of the development and interdisciplinary themes, we consider how differences in both the measurement of sex typing and the conceptualization of gender identity across different disciplinary fields may lead researchers to different conclusions regarding their implications for well-being. To this end, we examine how researchers have historically thought about the connection between gender identity, adherence to gender norms, and adjustment outcomes. We will also examine the ways in which researchers have measured adherence to gender norms and why it is important to conceive of sex typing as the product of both individual differences and normative developmental processes.

NEW DIRECTIONS FOR CHILD AND ADOLESCENT DEVELOPMENT • DOI: 10.1002/cd

Typically sex typing has been studied from either an individual or nor-mative difference point of view; these perspectives have rarely been consid-ered together. Social psychologists have generally focused on documenting individual differences in sex typing in adulthood (Bem, 1974). In contrast, developmental psychologists have mostly concentrated on understanding normative changes in sex typing, particularly those occurring during early childhood (Kagan, 1964; Kohlberg, 1966). However, individual and norma-tive differences in sex typing are relevant throughout the life span. A primary theme in the analysis here is that the impact of individual and normative dif-ferences on adjustment differs in accordance with developmental phases. In particular, we explore how individual and normative differences in sex typ-ing affect adjustment differently during early and middle childhood.

To address the intersection-of-identities theme, we consider the implica-tions of recognizing gender identity as multidimensional for the relationship between social identity and personal adjustment. Multidimensionality may be conceptualized in a variety of ways, but broadly it refers to the idea that social identity reflects knowledge of group membership along with a variety of beliefs about group membership (Ashmore, Deaux, & McLaughlin-Volpe, 2004). Thus, gender identity may be conceptualized as both categorical knowledge ("I'm a boy/girl") and feelings regarding the importance ("Being a boy/girl is really important to me") and evaluation ("I like being a boy/girl") of that group membership. This perspective has been shown to be important for understand-ing the impact of both racial and gender identity on adjustment (Egan & Perry, 2001; Sellers, Smith, Shelton, Rowley, & Chavous, 1998; Brown & Tappan, Chapter Four). In the discussion, we aim to advance the idea that the mean-ing individuals ascribe to their gender identity is critically important for under-standing the relationship between adherence to gender norms and well-being.

Historical Perspective on Gender Identity, Sex Typing, and Adjustment

Initially developmental psychologists defined gender identity as the extent to which an individual feels masculine or feminine. Feeling masculine or feminine was assumed to be important to children and to depend on adher-ence to cultural standards of masculinity or femininity. In essence, it was believed that the presence of sex typing was necessary for possessing a secure sense of self as male or female. Moreover, researchers thought that individuals whose behavior matched sex role prescriptions were more likely to be psychologically well adjusted because they would be fulfilling a psy-chological need to conform to internalized cultural standards of gender. Thus, sex typing was viewed as not only normal but optimal, whereas cross-sex typing was viewed as deviant and potentially harmful to well-being (Kagan, 1964). Bem (1974, 1981), however, challenged this perspective, arguing that the need to adhere to an internalized standard of gender would promote negative, not positive, adjustment.

NEW DIRECTIONS FOR CHILD AND ADOLESCENT DEVELOPMENT • DOI: 10.1002/cd

Unlike Kagan (1964), who attributed the development of sex typing in part to identification with the same-sex parent, Bem (1981) believed that sex typing resulted from the salient and functional use of gender in society. Specifically Bem thought that societal gender distinctions led people to develop gender schemas, or associative mental networks linking certain behaviors to either men or women. The contents of these schemas were theorized to function as standards people would use to evaluate whether they were adequate representations of their gender group. Thus for Bem, the extent to which people were sex typed was indicative of the extent to which they were gender schematic or had internalized culturally prescribed gender norms. So although Bem agreed that people were motivated to adhere to internalized cultural standards of gender, in contrast to Kagan, she believed that this tendency would result in behavioral inflexibility and therefore maladjustment. (Subsequent support for Bem's idea that androgyny is associated with better adjustment has been mixed. Thus, the extent to which androgyny is beneficial for adjustment remains unclear. See Ruble & Martin, 1998, for further discussion.)

Although subsequent research (Spence & Helmreich, 1980) critiqued Bem's assessment of masculinity/femininity, Bem's perspective (1974, 1981) has influenced developmental and social psychologists in a number of ways. Specifically, Bem, along with other researchers (Liben & Signorella, 1980; Martin & Halverson, 1981), popularized the notion of gender schemata as a key mechanism promoting the development of sex-typed behavior. To this day, the construct of gender schemata remains highly important to cognitive theories of gender development (Martin, Ruble, & Szkrybalo, 2002; Ruble, Martin, & Berenbaum, 2006). Moreover, Bem pioneered the practice of measuring masculinity and femininity separately, operationalizing the concept of androgyny and influencing later theorizing about the implications of sex typing. Bem's assertion that sex typing is maladaptive and ultimately serves to restrict people's behaviors inspired numerous studies and changed the way in which researchers framed the relationship between sex typing and adjustment, with sex role flexibility becoming the optimal standard (Ruble & Martin, 1998). Yet, the relationship of gender identity, sex typing, and adjustment may not be as straightforward as Bem theorized.

Sex Typing: Individual Versus Normative Differences

Bem's (1981) perspective on the potentially negative consequences of being highly sex typed is primarily based on analyses relating individual differences in sex typing to adjustment. Specifically, Bem (1974) identified individuals as highly sex typed by measuring the extent to which they reported possessing more same-sex compared to opposite-sex traits. Although this method of quantifying differences in sex typing is legitimate, it treats sex typing as a relatively stable characteristic without regard to its developmental context. That is, across development, children may differ relative to each other (for example, child X is more sex typed than child Y) and to themselves in terms of sex typing (child X is more sex typed at age five than at age three). Indeed, for many decades, developmental psychologists have devoted considerable attention to documenting normative changes in sex typing.

In one of the most influential works on the mechanisms underlying the adoption of sex-typed behavior in children, Kohlberg (1966) theorized that knowledge of one's gender category membership ("I am a boy/girl") and the achievement of gender constancy ("Boys will grow up to be men; a boy is still a boy even if he wears a dress") are critical components underlying the expression of sex-typed beliefs and behaviors. Although Kohlberg's ideas remain controversial (see Bandura & Bussey, 2004; Bussey & Bandura, 1999), they continue to influence how developmental researchers think about the relationship between sex typing and gender identity (see Martin et al., 2002). It is important to note that while both Kohlberg and Bem's (1981) theories presume that gender identity and sex typing are inherently linked, Kohlberg was mostly interested in the relationship between gender identity and sex typing in childhood, whereas Bem was primarily concerned with the implications of sex typing for adjustment among adults. Following in Kohlberg's footsteps, cognitive developmental researchers have generally directed their efforts toward documenting a relationship between gender knowledge ("I'm a boy/girl") and age-related increases in sex typing. Similarly, developmental researchers interested in gender schemata have generally been more concerned with understanding how children construct their schemata and whether this leads to increases in sex typing. Neither approach has given much consideration to how potentially rigid sex typing affects adjustment (Martin et al., 2002; Ruble et al., 2006). Perhaps this is because rigidity in children's beliefs and behaviors in general has long been recognized as a hallmark of development and consequently has not generally been viewed as especially problematic for adjustment.

Numerous theoretical and empirical analyses suggest that differences in the flexibility versus rigidity of individuals' sex-typed beliefs reflect not only individual differences in beliefs about gender norms but also normative developmental trajectories. For example, Ruble (1994) suggests that as children come to understand that gender is an important social category, their beliefs about gender progress through three phases. During the initial phase, construction, children are mostly concerned with seeking gender-relevant information and, due to their possession of a relatively incomplete amount of gender knowledge, will not react strongly to gender norm violations. In contrast, during the second phase, consolidation, children have a well-developed set of gender stereotypes and exhibit a peak in the rigidity of their gender beliefs. In the final phase, integration, children apply gender-related information more flexibly compared to the previous phase and may show individual differences in their gender cognitions and schemata.

The results from a recent longitudinal study support these assertions. In this study, children showed a peak in the rigidity of their application of gender stereotypes at five or six years, but by age seven began to show dramatic increases in flexibility. In addition, regardless of the level of rigidity between five and seven years, children previously high or low in rigidity showed no differences in flexibility by age eight, suggesting that this pattern of early rigidity followed by increasing flexibility represents a normative developmental process (Trautner et al., 2005).

Multidimensionality of Gender Identity

Although Kagan (1964) and Bem (1981) differed in terms of the mechanisms believed to promote sex typing and whether or not sex typing is adaptive or maladaptive, both perspectives posit that sex typing is indicative of gender identity. Although it is not an unreasonable idea, recent work examining the nature of identity suggests that it may be much more complex than the degree to which people adhere to gender norms. Contemporary perspectives on identity challenge the utility of relying on one construct or type of measurement as a means for assessing the nature of a particular identity (Ashmore et al., 2004; Egan & Perry, 2001; Sellers et al., 1998; Way, Santos, Niwa, Kim-Gervey, Chapter Five). Specifically, researchers have proposed that social identities are made up of various components, each with important implications for particular outcomes (Ruble et al., 2004). Although psychologists differ in the aspects of identity they emphasize, current research points to three dimensions worth careful consideration when thinking about gender identity, sex typing, and adjustment: centrality, evaluation, and felt pressure. (Centrality refers to the importance of gender to one's identity; evaluation refers to how one views gender-related values, beliefs, roles, and behavioral practices in one's culture; and felt pressure refers to one's perceptions of the need to conform to these cultural values, beliefs, roles, and behavioral practices.)

Although gender may be among the most important social categories in American society, individuals may differ in the degree to which they consider it an important and positive aspect of their overall identity. Research has shown that children differ in predictable ways with respect to which aspects of their overall identity they consider most important. For example, ethnicity is more central to the self-concept of immigrant compared to non-immigrant American children. Moreover, research has shown that children may differ in the extent to which they are happy with their gender and feel pressure from themselves and others (parents and peers) to behave in a sex-typed manner. Thus, centrality, evaluation, and felt pressure have all been shown to be important factors in the relationship between group membership and self-esteem (Ruble et al., 2004).

Our Study

Recent work in our lab has been directed toward considering the impact of children's rigid sex-typed beliefs from individual difference, developmental, and multidimensional perspectives. Specifically we examined whether the implications of rigid sex-typed beliefs for adjustment differed depending on whether we (1) conceptualized children's rigid sex-typed beliefs as reflecting individual or normative differences and (2) considered the extent to which children regard gender as a central and positive aspect of their self-concept. Although a peak in rigidity is a hallmark of the consolidation phase, children may nevertheless vary in the degree to which they exhibit rigid sex-typed beliefs. Moreover, the impact of individual differences in rigidity may differ depending on whether children are highly rigid relative to their peers prior to or after reaching peak rigidity. The impact of rigid sex-typed beliefs on adjustment may also vary depending on whether children perceive their gender group membership as an important and positive aspect of themselves.

To explore these issues, we conducted interviews with children at two different time points. At time 1, children ($n = 95$) were between three and seven years of age ($M = 5.14$), and at wave 2 ($n = 59$), they were between seven and thirteen years of age ($M = 10.27$). The overwhelming majority of participants were white, precluding us from examining any differences by ethnicity. At both time points, we measured children's sex role rigidity by assessing their reactions to other children's gender norm violations (a girl [boy] who plays with trucks [dolls]), feelings of gender centrality ("Being a girl is a big part of who I am"), and evaluation ("I am proud to be a girl") (see Ruble et al., 2007, for a full description of these measures), and global self-worth (Harter, 1985). We decided to measure rigidity in this way primarily because Bem's (1974) measures have not been adapted for preschool children, and children's reactions to gender norm violations are a plausible indicator of the extent to which they have internalized culturally prescribed gender norms.

Individual and Normative Differences. To identify periods before and after peak rigidity, we created smoothed Loess plots with age as the independent variable and sex role rigidity as the dependent variable. Inspection of the plots demonstrated the familiar curvilinear pattern of children showing a peak in sex role rigidity around five years followed by a decline shortly after (see Figure 3.1). To account for these different trends in the data, we divided participants at time 1 into younger (3.13–4.99) ($n = 42$) and older (5.00–7.30) ($n = 53$) cohorts as a way of designating times before and after peak rigidity, respectively.

We approached the following time analysis with two questions in mind: (1) Does the relationship between rigidity and adjustment differ depending on whether children exhibit rigid sex-typed beliefs before or after reaching peak rigidity? and (2) Is the high rigidity exhibited in younger versus older children less stable? For each question, we predicted that heightened rigidity at time 1 (T1) would be related to adjustment and predict later rigidity, but only when it represented a departure from developmental norms (that is, it was exhibited after peak rigidity).

Although these predictions may appear to conflict with Bem's (1981) stance that rigidity is associated with poorer adjustment, fluctuations in the rigidity of children's beliefs reflect a normative developmental process. Thus,

Figure 3.1. Loess Plot for Age and Sex Role Rigidity at Time 1

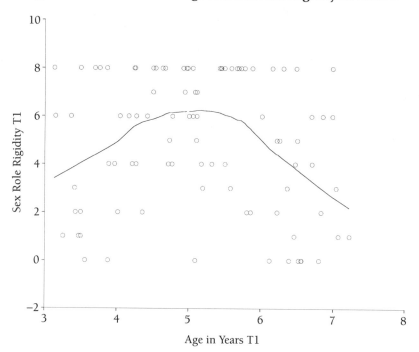

we might expect heightened rigidity to be problematic, but only when it represents a departure from developmental norms (that is, it is exhibited after peak rigidity). In addition, whereas heightened rigidity among younger children is consistent with normative increases in the rigidity of sex-typed beliefs, heightened rigidity among older children is out of sync with normative decreases in rigidity. Thus, the effects of heightened rigidity may be relatively short-lived when children are highly rigid before compared to after peak rigidity.

To answer our first question, we examined whether the relationship between rigidity and adjustment differed for younger and older children. Results from our first analysis confirmed that the effect of sex role rigidity on adjustment differed depending on whether children had reached peak rigidity. For participants in the younger cohort, who are unlikely to have reached peak rigidity, sex role rigidity appeared to have little impact on self-worth. However, consistent with Bem's theory (1981), for participants in the older cohort, who should have already reached peak rigidity, sex role rigidity was negatively associated with self-worth. This basic pattern of results remained the same in a follow-up analysis in which we adjusted for age-related differences in rigidity.

To investigate our second question, we conducted separate analyses for each cohort to examine whether participants' level of sex role rigidity at time 1 was associated with their level of sex role rigidity at time 2. Because participants were interviewed at time 2 anywhere from approximately 3.5 to 6.0 years after time 1, we adjusted for the length of time between interviews. For the younger cohort, there was no relationship between rigidity at time 1 and rigidity at time 2. However, for the older cohort, high rigidity at time 1 predicted high rigidity at time 2. These results make sense in the light of the previous analyses. Specifically, if individual differences in rigidity prior to peak rigidity are relatively fleeting, it seems reasonable that they may not relate to adjustment. Similarly, for the older cohort, if individual differences in rigidity after peak rigidity represent a more stable difference, we might expect this to have a significant impact on adjustment.

Because there are normative developmental changes in the older as well as the younger cohort, it may seem surprising that we found a relationship between rigidity and adjustment for the older cohort. One explanation is that although becoming highly rigid is a normal part of development, the briefer the time during which children are at their peak rigidity or the steeper the decline in peak rigidity, the better. One possible reason for this is that the longer or the later children show rigidity, the greater the overlap is between their rigid insistence on adherence to gender norms and the first years of elementary school, when peer relationships become more complex and require a wider range of social skills. Thus, consistent with Bem's (1981) ideas regarding the detrimental effects of rigidity, children who remain rigid for longer may miss out on opportunities to develop certain skills associated with the opposite sex (for example, girls learning to be assertive, boys learning to be cooperative) that may be beneficial for adjustment. In addition, after reaching peak rigidity, the extent to which children are high in rigidity relative to each other may be related to other types of gender-related individual differences (say, the extent to which children feel pressured to adhere to gender norms) and more general social cognitive differences (such as understanding others' mental states) that might be important for adjustment.

Heightened rigidity is also developmentally appropriate for younger children, whereas for older children, it represents a departure from developmental norms, and thus may have significant consequences for peer relationships and therefore adjustment. For example, because young children as a group are generally intolerant of gender norm violations, they likely share their maintenance of gender boundaries with other children, which may help to promote peer relationships. However, older children who are less tolerant of departures from gender norms are probably more of a minority among similar-age peers and therefore may be viewed as unfriendly or mean. Thus, we believe our results suggest that it is important to consider not only whether an individual holds rigid sex-typed beliefs relative to others but also the timing and stability of such differences.

Centrality/Evaluation and Felt Pressure.   To explore whether the relationship between sex typing and adjustment depends on the extent to which participants consider gender an important and positive aspect of their identities, we conducted another series of analyses with data from time 1. Because the results from our previous analyses showed that the impact of individual differences in sex role rigidity depended on whether participants were showing greater differences before or after peak rigidity, analyses were conducted separately for each cohort. For analyses of both the younger and older cohorts, we examined the relationship of self-worth, sex, sex role rigidity, and centrality/evaluation.

Consistent with our previous results, no significant effects emerged for the younger cohort. However, for the older cohort, results showed that high sex role rigidity was negatively associated with self-worth, but only when centrality/evaluation was also low (see Figure 3.2). In other words, children who had more rigid beliefs about how girls or boys should behave had lower levels of self-worth, but only if gender was not an important part of their identities. We speculate that these results make sense if we consider that centrality/evaluation may also reflect the extent to which individuals embrace the values and behaviors for their gender group. Thus, we would not necessarily expect high sex role rigidity to be bad for adjustment for those high in centrality/evaluation because adhering to gender norms may be congruent with personal standards of behavior. However, if individuals do not embrace gender norms yet have rigid beliefs about how they should

Figure 3.2 Predicted Values for Self-Worth as a Function of Sex Role Rigidity and Centrality/Evaluation for Participants in the Older Cohort

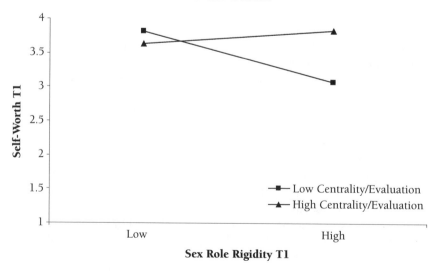

conform to them, it seems plausible that such a combination would be associated with negative adjustment.

Results from the second wave (time 2) of data collection are relevant to this point: although sex role rigidity was positively associated with felt pressure ("I think my parents would mind if I wanted to do things that only girls [boys] do"), centrality/evaluation was not. The lack of relationship between centrality/evaluation and felt pressure suggests that embracing and valuing the behaviors of one's gender group is distinct from pressure to adhere to gender norms. These results are in line with distinctions made by other researchers (Egan & Perry, 2001) between felt compatibility with one's gender group and felt pressure to adhere to gender norms. Moreover, our data are consistent with the spirit of Bem's (1981) theory, which implies that the pressure felt as a consequence of needing to match behaviors to an internalized standard of gender may be problematic. Importantly, research shows that felt pressure is associated with lower levels of self-worth in both middle childhood (Egan & Perry, 2001) and early adolescence (Smith & Leaper, 2005).

We should also point out that although we did not find different patterns for boys and girls in terms of the impact of sex typing on adjustment in either set of analyses, such differences may emerge later in life. Specifically, in a study with high school students, results showed that in the public context of school, feminine girls experienced greater loss of voice, expressing their opinions less, compared to androgynous girls. Boys showed a different pattern in that masculine boys reported higher levels of voice with male classmates compared to androgynous boys, who in turn reported higher levels of voice with close friends compared to masculine boys. Importantly, loss of voice is associated with lower levels of self-worth. Thus, these differences between girls and boys regarding their level of voice suggest that the impact of sex typing on adjustment may differ by gender during different developmental periods and across different contexts (Harter, Waters, Whitesell, & Kastelic, 1998).

Conclusion

Throughout this chapter, we have suggested that the relationship of sex typing, gender identity, and adjustment may not be as straightforward as prior theories have suggested. Specifically, we have proposed that in order to clarify the relationship of these constructs, it is important to consider individual differences in sex typing within the context of normative developmental processes and the multidimensional nature of gender identity. We believe our results have important implications for the main themes of this volume: (1) processes of identity development, (2) the intersection of personal and social identities, and (3) interdisciplinarity in social identity research.

With respect to developmental processes, our longitudinal analyses indicate that the stability and consequences of social (gender) identity may differ dramatically for children who are pre- versus post-peak rigidity. For

NEW DIRECTIONS FOR CHILD AND ADOLESCENT DEVELOPMENT • DOI: 10.1002/cd

example, individual differences in sex role rigidity showed stability over time and related to self-esteem only for children past peak rigidity. These findings raise interesting questions and have important theoretical implications for how we understand the consequences of sex typing. Specifically, what is it about the developmental period after peak rigidity that contributes to the greater stability and impact of sex typing on adjustment? As we suggested, one possibility concerns changing values and standards for children's peer relationships and interactions. However, many other possibilities exist, and it will be important for future research to examine more precisely those factors underlying the different patterns and implications of social identity across development. In addition, theories about the significance of individual differences in sex typing will need to ground their analyses more carefully in terms of normative developmental processes.

With respect to the intersection of personal and social identity, our results suggest that the nature of children's thinking about their gender group membership is far richer than has traditionally been recognized, in ways that are important for connecting various outgrowths of their gender identity (sex typing) to their self-concept and self-esteem. Specifically, our data suggest that it is not only the degree to which children adhere to gender norms, but also the extent to which they consider gender an important or positive aspect of their self-concept that predicts well-being. How the multidimensional nature of gender identity affects children's overall self-concept is an interesting issue. For example, will the self-concept of children for whom gender is a less central and less positive aspect of their identity be more resistant to gender stereotypes? More specifically, when encountering gender stereotypes such as, "girls are bad at math" or "boys play rough," will girls and boys who consider gender neither important nor positive be less likely to infer that they will be bad at math or should play rough, respectively? In addition, the feelings of importance and evaluation children ascribe to their gender seem like plausible mechanisms for promoting the development of sex segregation—the child-driven phenomenon in which children prefer to exclusively play with same-sex peers—which in turn may influence the areas children identify as relevant bases for their self-concept (looking feminine versus being good at sports).

Consideration of how gender identity intersects with other identities like ethnicity or class is important for fully understanding the ramifications of sex typing for adjustment (see Chapter Four, this volume). Unfortunately, the makeup of our sample did not allow us to explore differences in gender identity across ethnicity and class. However, it is important that future research explore the ways in which children's gender identities differ in concert with various combinations of ethnic and class identities. Variations by ethnicity and class in the ways in which people define gender could also have important implications for the relationship between sex typing and adjustment. For example, in their study of an ethnically diverse, low-income sample of adolescent boys, Santos, Way, and Hughes (2007) found that boys who adhered more to norms of masculinity had lower self-esteem. On the one hand, this finding makes sense because masculinity stresses a variety of antisocial behaviors such as physical aggression. However, many socially adaptive behaviors, such as assertiveness, define masculinity as well. The same can be said for femininity as it is defined by both potentially adaptive (nurturance) and maladaptive (submissiveness) behaviors. But what determines whether children use adaptive or maladaptive aspects of gender to define what it means to be a boy or a girl? One possibility is that children from different ethnic and socioeconomic groups define being a girl or a boy differently. For example, research shows that gender roles and concepts differ across ethnic and socioeconomic groups (Ruble et al., 2006). Thus, children from different ethnic and socioeconomic groups may have different ideas about what it means to be a boy or a girl and therefore vary in the extent to which they subscribe to adaptive or maladaptive aspects of masculinity or femininity. In short, it seems likely that the consequences of rigid adherence to gender norms differ in accordance with children's gender, ethnic, and socioeconomic group memberships.

In addition, it is important to consider the context in which children derive meaning from their gender identity. For example, in a high school in which Puerto Rican students were at the top of the social pecking order, Puerto Rican students felt positive about their ethnic identity. In contrast, Chinese students, who ranked at the bottom of the social hierarchy, felt much less positive about their ethnic identity. Interestingly, Dominican students, who ranked second highest in the social hierarchy, negotiated their ethnic identities in reference to the stereotypes conferred on them by their more dominant Puerto Rican peers. Thus, context affected how adolescents felt about their ethnic identity as well as how they defined it (Chapter Five, this volume).

With respect to interdisciplinarity in research on identity, we have employed both social and developmental perspectives in our work. In this chapter, we have argued that consideration of both individual and normative differences in sex typing, along with the recognition of gender identity as a multidimensional construct, is essential for understanding the relationship between sex typing and adjustment. However, despite a plethora of theoretical models positing important changes throughout life, developmental psychologists, for a variety of reasons, have primarily concerned themselves with childhood and adolescence, and social psychologists have primarily focused on adulthood (Ruble & Goodnow, 1998). An integrative interdisciplinary perspective forces us to study people across the life span and recognize the social and developmental factors relevant to the study of identity at all ages.

An interdisciplinary life span perspective seems ripe for exploration as empirical work shows that when adopting a new identity, both children and adults display the same curvilinear pattern of increasing rigidity of beliefs followed by later flexibility (Ruble, 1994). However, the extent to which adults may show a pattern similar to what our data show for children is an open question. Some research demonstrates an increase in gender traditionality during middle and late adolescence, suggesting that the intensity of sex typing continues to fluctuate well beyond childhood (Crouter, Whiteman, McHale, & Osgood, 2007). Thus, examining whether the intensity of sex typing continues to wax and wane throughout adulthood may represent a potentially fruitful line of inquiry. For instance, the relationship between sex typing and adjustment may differ across the life span because rigid sex-typed beliefs and behaviors during elementary school may manifest themselves in ways that are less directly related to adjustment (for example, believing that only girls should play with dolls) compared to high school or college (for example, believing that only men should be assertive and that women are less skilled at math). Furthermore, developmental and contextual differences in centrality, evaluation, and felt pressure may work to influence the relationship between sex typing and adjustment. For example, as girls begin to recognize that femininity is devalued relative to masculinity in American culture, the extent to which they believe being a girl is an important or positive aspect of their identity may decline. In addition, felt pressure to adhere to gender norms may be particularly detrimental for girls who feel pressure to be feminine but recognize that American culture grants less power and status to femininity (see also Chapter Four, this volume).

A developmental perspective on social identity and adjustment will also be enriched by a greater incorporation of social psychologists' emphasis on process. That is, what exactly is it about rigidity that may result in poor adjustment? Bem (1981) explicitly stated that rigid adherence to gender norms interferes with the ability to react adaptively across situations, especially when the required behavior violates gender norms. However, the data used to support this claim only suggest that sex-typed individuals are uncomfortable stepping outside their gender role (Bem & Lenney, 1976). Such an explanation for the consequences of rigidity seems incomplete. People may be rigidly sex typed but for different reasons, and these reasons might hold different implications for developmental outcomes. For example, some people may rigidly adhere to gender norms because they want to avoid negative outcomes related to violating gender norms (for example, wearing a feminine outfit to avoid being criticized for being unfeminine or looking unattractive), while others may want to maximize the positive benefits associated with being gendered (for example, wearing a feminine outfit because of a desire to be admired for being feminine and perceived as attractive). This distinction is consistent with the two primary motivational orientations described in regulatory focus theory, an influential social psychological theory. This theory posits that people can be described as being either prevention or promotion focused. While individuals with a prevention focus are particularly concerned with avoiding negative outcomes, individuals with a promotion focus are concerned with obtaining positive outcomes (Higgins, 2000). According to this theory, differences in regulatory focus may foster different motives for engaging in gender normative behavior. For example, we might expect prevention-focused women to insist on wearing a feminine outfit because they do not want to be socially rejected, whereas promotion-focused women may be primarily concerned with gaining social acceptance. People with different orientations may react quite differently when forced to step outside their gender role, which may be important for understanding the relationship between sex typing and adjustment.

In conclusion, our findings suggest that the relationship of sex typing, gender identity, and adjustment is not as straightforward as originally believed. Both the timing and degree of rigidity deserve consideration when examining the relationship between sex typing and adjustment. Furthermore, our data demonstrate that, consistent with contemporary theories of identity, the multidimensional nature of gender identity has important implications for the circumstances under which sex typing may be adaptive versus maladaptive. Rather than asking whether sex typing and gender identity are good or bad for adjustment, we encourage researchers to revisit previous conclusions about the nature of the relationship of sex typing, gender identity, and adjustment, keeping in mind the diverse ways in which they may be conceptualized and relate to each other.

References

Ashmore, R. D., Deaux, K., & McLaughlin-Volpe, T. (2004). An organizing framework for collective identity: Articulation and significance of multidimensionality. *Psychological Bulletin, 130,* 80–114.

Bandura, A., & Bussey, K. (2004). On broadening the cognitive, motivational, and sociocultural scope of theorizing about gender development and functioning: Comment on Martin, Ruble, and Szkrybalo (2002). *Psychological Bulletin, 130,* 691–701.

Bem, S. L. (1974). The measurement of psychological androgyny. *Journal of Consulting and Clinical Psychology, 42,* 155–162.

Bem, S. L. (1981). Gender schema theory: A cognitive account of sex typing. *Psychological Review, 88,* 354–364.

Bem, S. L., & Lenney, E. (1976). Sex typing and the avoidance of cross-sex behavior. *Journal of Personality and Social Psychology, 33,* 48–54.

Bussey, K., & Bandura, A. (1999). Social cognitive theory of gender development and differentiation. *Psychological Review, 106,* 676–713.

Crouter, A. C., Whiteman, S. D., McHale, S. M., & Osgood, W. D. (2007). Development of gender attitude traditionality across middle childhood and adolescence. *Child Development, 78,* 911–926.

Egan, S. K., & Perry, D. G. (2001). Gender identity: A multidimensional analysis with implications for psychosocial adjustment. *Developmental Psychology, 37,* 451–463.

Harter, S. (1985). *The Self-Perception Profile for Children: Revision of the perceived competence scale for children (Manual).* Denver, CO: University of Denver.

Harter, S., Waters, P. L., Whitesell, N. R., & Kastelic, D. (1998). Level of voice among female and male high school students: Relational context, support, and gender orientation. *Developmental Psychology, 34,* 892–901.

Higgins, E. T. (2000). Making a good decision: Value from fit. *American Psychologist, 55,* 1217–1230.

Kagan, J. (1964) A cognitive-developmental analysis of children's sex-role concepts and attitudes. In M. L. Hoffman & L. W. Hoffman (Eds.), *Review of child development research* (Vol. 1, pp. 137–167). New York: Russell Sage Foundation.

Kohlberg, L. A. (1966). A cognitive-developmental analysis of children's sex role concepts and attitudes. In E. E. Maccoby (Ed.), *The development of sex differences* (pp. 82–173). Stanford, CA: Stanford University Press.

Liben, L. S., & Signorella, M. L. (1980). Gender-related schemata and constructive memory in children. *Child Development, 51,* 11–18.

Martin, C. L., & Halverson, C. (1981). A schematic processing model of sex typing and stereotyping in children. *Child Development, 52,* 1119–1134.

Martin, C. L., Ruble, D. N., & Szkrybalo, J. (2002). Cognitive theories of early gender development. *Psychological Bulletin, 128,* 903–933.

Ruble, D. N. (1994). A phase model of transitions: Cognitive and motivational consequences. In M. Zanna (Ed.), *Advances in experimental social psychology, 26,* 163–214.

Ruble, D. N., Alvarez, J. M., Bachman, M., Cameron, J. A., Fuligni, A. J., Garcia Coll, C., et al. (2004). The development of a sense of "we": The emergence and implications of children's collective identity. In M. Bennett & F. Sani (Eds.), *The development of the social self* (pp. 29–76). East Sussex, England: Psychology Press.

Ruble, D. N., & Goodnow, J. (1998). Social development from a lifespan perspective. In D. Gilbert, S. Fiske, & G. Lindzey (Eds.), *Handbook of social psychology.* New York: McGraw-Hill.

Ruble, D. N., & Martin, C. (1998). Gender development. In W. Damon (Series Ed.) & N. Eisenberg (Vol. Ed.), *Handbook of child psychology: Vol. 3, Social, emotional, and personality development* (5th ed., pp. 933–1016). Hoboken, NJ: Wiley.

Ruble, D. N., Martin, C. L., & Berenbaum, S. A. (2006). Gender development. In W. Damon (Series Ed.) & N. Eisenberg (Vol. Ed.), *Handbook of child psychology: Vol. 3, Social, emotional, and personality development* (6th ed., pp. 858–932). Hoboken, NJ: Wiley.

Ruble, D. N., Taylor, L., Cyphers, L., Greulich, F., K., Lurye, L. E., & Shrout, P. E. (2007). The role of gender constancy in early gender development. *Child Development, 78,* 1121–1136.

Santos, C., Way, N., & Hughes, D. (2007, April). *Patterns of adherence to norms of masculinity in the peer relationships of multi-ethnic adolescent boys.* Poster session presented at the Society for Research in Child Development 2007 Biennial Meeting, Boston.

Sellers, R. M., Smith, M., Shelton, J. N., Rowley, S.A.J., & Chavous, T. M. (1998). Multidimensional model of racial identity: A reconceptualization of African American racial identity. *Personality and Social Psychology Review, 2,* 18–39.

Smith, T. E., & Leaper, C. (2005). Self-perceived gender typicality and the peer context during adolescence. *Journal of Research on Adolescence, 16,* 91–103.

Spence, J. T., & Helmreich, R. L. (1980). Masculine instrumentality and feminine expressiveness: Their relationships with sex role attitudes and behaviors. *Psychology of Women Quarterly, 5,* 147–163.

Trautner, H. M., Ruble, D. N., Cyphers, L., Kirsten, B., Behrendt, R., & Hartmann, P. (2005). Rigidity and flexibility of gender stereotypes in children: Developmental or differential? *Infant and Child Development, 14,* 365–380.

LEAH E. LURYE *is a doctoral student at New York University, New York.*

KRISTINA M. ZOSULS *is a doctoral student at New York University, New York.*

DIANE N. RUBLE *is professor of psychology at New York University, New York.*

Brown, L. M., & Tappan, M. B. (2008). Fighting like a girl fighting like a guy: Gender identity, ideology, and girls at early adolescence. In M. Azmitia, M. Syed, & K. Radmacher
(Eds.), *The intersections of personal and social identities. New Directions for Child and Adolescent Development, 120,* 47–59.

4

Fighting Like a Girl Fighting Like a Guy: Gender Identity, Ideology, and Girls at Early Adolescence

Lyn Mikel Brown, Mark B. Tappan

Abstract

*In this chapter we explore the phenomenon of "girls fighting like guys" by lis-
tening to adolescent girls' justification for physical fighting with other girls. We
argue that physical girlfighting is a particular kind of gendered performance—
a performance of identity that expresses, at least in part, an answer to the question, "Who am I?"—that both perpetuates and challenges the usual notions of
masculinity and femininity and the differential power associated with these discourses. We present a sociocultural approach to identity that we believe not only
holds promise for helping us to understand girl-fighting behavior but also highlights the clear interrelationship between social identity and personal identity.
We conclude by highlighting several implications of this analysis for those who
work with girls (and boys) in educational and clinical settings.* © Wiley Periodicals, Inc.

irlfighting has always been popular in the media. A good public girl-fight makes for a sensationalized news story, especially if photos or video are available. There has long been public obsession with erotically tinged violence in female prison movies, mud- or gelatin-wrestling matches, and pornography magazines. While catfights still provide plenty of tension release and humor in movies and sitcoms, increasingly female martial arts experts, weapons-toting fantasy characters, and angry women seeking vengeance have taken center stage.

As girl power in the form of strength and physical prowess has made its way into popular culture, so has increased concern about female aggression. Are girls becoming more like guys, taking on their most troublesome violent behaviors? While some celebrate the birth of the tough girl in media and in real life, others worry about the consequences: girl gangs and girl-on-girl aggression on school playgrounds and after-school hangouts. Still others raise concerns about the eroticized femininity that accompanies media female fighters and the fact that female anger and aggression are most likely directed at other girls and women.

In this chapter we explore the phenomenon of girls fighting like guys more closely by listening to adolescent girls' justification for physical fighting with other girls and by examining media depictions of violent girlfights. We argue that physical girlfighting is less about adopting male behaviors than it is about redefining what it means to be a girl living in a patriarchal culture. As such, girlfighting is a particular kind of gendered performance—a performance of identity that expresses, at least in part, an answer to the question, "Who am I?"—that both perpetuates and challenges the usual notions of masculinity and femininity and the differential power associated with these discourses. It also illustrates well, we argue, the degree to which personal identity is always mediated by social identity.

We begin with a reflection on the public perception of girl power and girlfighting and recent media depictions of girls' aggression. We turn to some examples from interviews and focus group conversations among seventh- and eighth-grade girls (ages twelve to fourteen) selected from studies of girls diverse with respect to social class, race, and ethnicity (Brown, 2003), to illustrate themes heard in girls' conversations about their physical fighting. We then present a sociocultural approach to identity (Brown, 1998; Tappan, 2000, 2005) that we believe not only holds promise for helping us to understand girl-fighting behavior, but also highlights the clear interrelationship between social identity and personal identity. We conclude by highlighting several implications of this analysis for those who work with girls (and boys) in educational and clinical settings.

The Power to Fight

The late 1980s and early 1990s witnessed heightened public anxiety about an increase in "bad girl" behavior in the form of girl gangs and physical violence, largely focusing on young women of color and citing radical increases in arrest and incarceration rates (Federal Bureau of Investigation, 1991, 2001). These increases were later proven to be overblown and misinterpreted, the result of newly criminalizing and relabeling minor offenses, with serious consequences, particularly for girls of color (Brown, Chesney-Lind, & Stein, 2007; Chesney-Lind & Irwin, 2007). But the image of the violent, aggressive bad girl, with all its racial and class stereotypes, signaled a public shift in the definition of femininity.

In the late 1990s, the Riot Grrl movement, a primarily white middle-class feminist do-it-yourself girl power movement, entered the public scene and further challenged such definitions. Celebrating all things girl through defiant punk bands, the reappropriation of *girlie,* and a network of underground zines (photocopied self-made magazines) where girls ranted about social injustice and sexism, Riot Grrls promised both personal and political change. As coverage of Riot Grrls made its way into mainstream media magazines, its message of fighting any form of girl-girl competition and advocating "girl love" became associated with a range of messages and products. Girl bands like the Spice Girls and movies like *Charlie's Angels* took up the girl power charge, redefining it as a sexualized, commodified, marketable concept (Aapola, Gonick, & Harris, 2005).

By the dawn of the new millennium, *girl power* had became a ubiquitous term, selling everything and anything girl related, often using the very stereotypes of feminine competition and jealousy the Riot Grrl movement meant to interrupt (see Lamb & Brown, 2006). Wealthy white girls became the new version of bad girls, and a spate of popular books defined and elevated concern about "mean girls" (Dellasega, 2003; Simmons, 2002; Talbot, 2002; Wiseman, 2003). As is so often the case, mainstream media followed suit, and soon a series of PG-13 movies targeting adolescent girls, such as *Mean Girls* and *Bring It On,* lampooned and reified the mean girl image. It was just a matter of time before the same messages could be found on popular TV sitcoms and pseudoreality shows like *The Simple Life, Laguna Beach,* and *My Super Sweet 16.* In just over a decade, concern about girls and violence shifted from the realities of negotiating racism and poverty to the prime-time spectacle of wealthy white girls competing for queen bee status.

More recently, in yet another twist, popular books and media have refocused attention on girls and physical aggression (Garbarino, 2006; Prothrow-Stith, Spivak, & Reno 2006). With critically acclaimed movies like *Girlfight* and *Million Dollar Baby,* TV shows like *Buffy the Vampire Slayer* and *Alias,* and the professional boxing legacies of Ali and Foreman passed down to daughters, physical fighting has a real presence in popular media and specifically in girls' popular culture. Indeed, Norma Feshbach's analysis (2005) of direct and indirect female aggression in TV sitcoms suggests that such aggression is now so common it has reached the status of a female character trait. Feshbach concludes that girls are now socialized into aggression through media.

What do we make of this very public display of so-called girl power? How do the images and messages both reflect and have an impact on girls' identities? Girlfighting is increasingly viewed as more than girls fighting "like girls," although there is a fair share of slapping, biting, and pulling hair in popular PG-13 movies. More often girls who take themselves seriously as fighters (in the movies and in real life) distance themselves from such "girlie" or "sissy" tactics and "fight like guys"—punching or taking other girls out and justifying their aggression using rationales and ideologies such as "protecting my territory," "demanding respect," or maintaining a "king of the hill" social hierarchy once reserved for boys and men (Brown, 2003).

Consider the very public hazing incident at a powder puff football game at Glenbrook High School in spring 2003. In this videotaped "savagery in the Chicago suburbs" (Meadows & Johnson, 2003), a group of privileged white senior high school girls kicked, punched, pushed, and beat junior girls with bats, and smeared them with pig intestines, feces, urine, fish guts, coffee grounds, and paint, all the while separating themselves from weak femininity by using misogynistic language to shame their victims into staying on the field—calling them "bitches," "wimps," and "sluts." In violent girlfights that show up regularly on YouTube or sites like PSF (Pure Street Fights), as well as in the popular DVD series "Extreme Chick Fights" sold through Amazon and other mainstream outlets, girls of all colors and social class backgrounds are labeled "extreme," "brutal," and "ass-kicking."

In the light of all this media attention on the subject and given our interest in the impact of girlfighting on girls' identity development and their sense of self-understanding, it seems important to consider how girls themselves talk about such physical girlfighting.

Three Examples from Fourteen-Year-Old Girls

According to Brandy, white and working class, "Girls can fight just as bad as boys, but they fight better, because they don't get the little wussy punches, you know, they really punch, girls do, they have the power." From Brandy's perspective, "Boys are soft-hearted. . . . Women in general are tougher. . . . I've noticed changes in a couple of my friends, they got more tough and are sticking up for themselves, not taking any guff from anybody."

Ruby, who is African American and working class, tells a story about getting in a fight with a girl in her neighborhood:

> It was me and my cousin and another friend of mine . . . and we were like [downtown] and so the girl was like, she was working [at a job], she's under-age and we went and told on her. So we came back and my cousin is the type of girl that likes to fight, so [Marti] was over there telling [my cousin], "Yah, your mother works the street," and arguing with her to get her mad. So then my cousin was like, "I can't fight her because then I will go back to [the youth center]." So she said, "Why don't you fight her?" And I wasn't in the mood

for fighting, so now she said something to aggravate me, so we sort of argued and then my cousin pushed her. . . . She fell down and she jumped up and hit me. . . . And I gave her my shot.

Ruby was not looking for a fight. She says she had to fight "because it's like, if you walk away you're chicken" and "because who is going to sit there as you talk about their mother and be calm? Nobody is going to." Laura, white and middle class, tells her story:

I got mad at [this girl] for giving my friend a cigarette, 'cause I don't want my friend to smoke. . . . I just went and I like tapped her on her shoulder 'cause she was standing in front of me and I was like "Why'd you give that person a cigarette?" and she like took me by my jacket, she threw me into the bulletin board and then she like got her knuckles out like that, and she punched me right in the chest and she left me there and I was like, my back was like "ow." It hurt really bad, and she just left me there and she started cussing me out, and then I was like, "You need to chill." And she's like, "You're pushing my limits," or whatever and "You need to back off." I was like, "I didn't do anything. It's what *you* did so just leave her alone."

While Brandy, Ruby, and Laura all describe incidents of physical fighting, their expression of anger and aggression, as well as the response these behaviors elicit in others, is affected by their social and material status and by the definitions of appropriate femininity communicated to them in their immediate communities through their families and friends. Any attempt to tease out gender as an organizing factor for these three girls must acknowledge the intersectionality of systems of oppression such as gender, class, and race (Crenshaw, 1995). As such, our analysis, although privileging gender, also has interfaces with both class and race.

Gender Identity as Mediated and Performed

To understand and make sense of these examples as gendered struggles, we employ an explicitly sociocultural approach to identity. From this perspective, identities are fundamentally forms of self-understanding: "people tell others who they are, but even more important, they tell themselves and then try to act as though they are who they say they are" (Holland, Lachicotte, Skinner, & Cain, 1998, p. 3). These self-understandings are not simply individual, internal, subjective conceptions of one's "essential self" rooted in the "core of one's being," that emerge from self-reflection, or as a result of the resolution of deeply seated intrapsychic conflicts or struggles (see Blasi, 1984). Rather, according to this view, identities are as much social as they are personal. In fact, they link the personal and the social: they entail action and interaction in a sociocultural context, they are social products lived in and through activity and practice (Holland et al., 1998), and they are performed and enacted (Butler, 1990, 1991).

NEW DIRECTIONS FOR CHILD AND ADOLESCENT DEVELOPMENT • DOI: 10.1002/cd

Following Penuel and Wertsch (1995), we have found it most helpful to view identity as a form of mediated action. The concept of mediated action entails two central elements: (1) an agent, the person who is doing the acting, and (2) the cultural tools, mediational means, or instruments appropriated from the culture and used by the agent to accomplish a given action (see also Rogoff, 1995; Tappan, 2000, 2005; Wertsch, 1998). Penuel and Wertsch (1995) connect Vygotsky's (1978) insights about developmental analysis, sociocultural processes, and mediation to Erik Erikson's (1968) insights about identity development in adolescence and young adulthood. While Erikson (1968), who defined identity as "a subjective sense of invigorating sameness and continuity" (p. 19), tended to emphasize individual functioning in his analysis of identity formation and Vygotsky tended to emphasize sociocultural processes in his analysis of developmental phenomena, it is possible, Penuel and Wertsch argue, to "integrate individual functioning and sociocultural processes" (p. 88) into a coherent approach to identity formation. That is, by seeking to maintain the dynamic tension that necessarily exists between the individual and society (a tension that both Vygotsky and Erikson recognized), an understanding of the role that social, cultural, and historical processes play in the formation and transformation of individual identities is not only possible but quite desirable.

Methodologically, adopting a mediated action approach to identity formation means focusing less on what people say about their own sense of self-understanding and more on what they do in specific situations and circumstances. In other words, the unit of analysis in such an approach is meaningful human action, not inner states or sociocultural processes. As such, the focus of attention is on how mediational means or cultural tools are used to construct identities in the course of specific activities and particular actions (Penuel & Wertsch, 1995).

The cultural and historical tools, resources, or mediational means that are most critical for identity formation, argue Penuel and Wertsch, are the ideologies that are available in, and appropriated from, a particular social-cultural-historical context. The meanings of these ideologies-used-as-cultural tools are not, however, fixed and immutable. Rather, these meanings are quite fluid and flexible, determined in large measure by how such resources and tools are used in a particular situation:

> The cultural and historical resources for identity formation do not constitute a single, undifferentiated whole, but represent a diversity of mediational means. In that way, identity may be conceived as formed when individuals choose on particular occasions to use one or more resources from a cultural "tool kit" to accomplish some action (see Bruner, 1990). Ideologies are embedded in a multitude of tools and signs; in this respect, identity researchers must be open to the variety of settings and signs in which an individual's identity is being constructed or expressed [Penuel and Wertsch, 1995, p. 90].

This conception of identity as mediated action links to feminist theorist Judith Butler's (1990, 1991) argument that identity is fundamentally performed or enacted (see also Goffman, 1959). Butler suggests, in particular, that identity is fragile, that the roles one plays are unstable, and hence, actors must continually repeat their performances of identity in different contexts and for different audiences in order to provide some measure of stability and certainty.

Fighting Like a Guy. So if identity is a form of mediated action that links the social to the personal, then it is performed or enacted (repeatedly, perhaps, in different contexts, for different audiences). Moreover, performance of one's identity necessarily entails the use of specific cultural tools and mediational means, particularly ideologies. To understand what the girls in our examples invoke or perform when they say things like, "girls can fight just as bad as boys," refer to "little wussy punches," say "girls have the power" or are "tough," accuse other girls' mothers of "working the street," say "I gave her my shot because if you walk away you're chicken," or "she got her knuckles out and punched me right in the chest and just left me there," we first need to understand what kinds of ideologies they have appropriated from their sociocultural context. One of the most salient appears to be an ideology, interestingly enough, that is typically linked to masculine social identity. This is what R. W. Connell (1987) terms *hegemonic masculinity*—that ideological constellation of ideas and attitudes that ensures male ascendancy "through a play of social forces that extends beyond contests of brute power into the organization of both private life and cultural processes" (p. 184). This masculine ideology typically includes attitudes about status ("a man always deserves the respect of his wife and children"), toughness ("A young man should be physically tough, even if he's not big"), and antifemininity ("It bothers me when a guy acts like a girl") (Pleck, Sonenstein, & Ku, 1993).

William Pollack's (1998) discussion of the "boy code" illustrates the way in which the ideology of hegemonic masculinity is encountered and appropriated by young boys. The "boy code," says Pollack, is "a set of behaviors, rules of conduct, cultural shibboleths, and even a lexicon" (p. xxv)—that is, a set of cultural tools and mediational means—that define the ways real boys should act and interact in the world:

> *The sturdy oak:* Boys and men should be stoic, stable and independent—do not share pain or grieve openly. Never show weakness—don't whimper, cry, or complain. Act like it doesn't hurt.
> *Give 'em hell:* Boys and men should exhibit extreme daring, bravado and attraction to violence. This stems from the myth that "boys will be boys."
> *The big wheel:* Boys and men should achieve status, dominance, and power; avoid shame at all costs; act cool and under control at all times.
> *No sissy stuff:* Boys and men should never express feelings (other than anger) or otherwise act in ways that might be seen as feminine.

This hegemonic masculine ideology represents a cultural resource that boys use to mediate their performance of masculine gender identity (see Tappan, 2001). It also represents, we would argue, a cultural resource that girls appropriate as well.

In their talk about physical fighting, girls show clear evidence that they too have appropriated hegemonic masculine ideology in ways that both help to reproduce it and ensure its dominance. Brandy's assertion that "boys are soft-hearted; women in general are tougher" invokes *the sturdy oak;* her statement that "girls can fight just as bad as boys" invokes *give 'em hell,* recasting a "boys will be boys" message to a "girls will be boys" message. When Ruby claims that "girls have the power" and accuses other girls' mothers of "working the street," she claims her power as a girl and ensures it by positioning herself within a masculine ideology, both through a misogynistic slur and by adopting a form of insult associated with African American boys. Her assertion, "I gave her my shot because if you walk away you're chicken," recalls the *big wheel* and its imperative to avoid shame at all costs. Brandy's reference to "little wussy punches" and Laura's recounting that "she got her knuckles out and punched me right in the chest and just left me there" in different ways appeal to *no sissy stuff.*

Fighting Like a Girl. Although masculine ideology is clearly an important aspect of the mediated, enacted identities of these girls, it is also important to acknowledge that when they fight, girls are appropriating what might be called an ideology of hegemonic femininity, which offers a different cultural resource and a different set of tools. This notion of what it means to fight like a girl pervades contemporary media. When fifteen-year-old Bahtya is asked about why there is so much fighting in her school, she says simply:

> It's the popular thing to do. TV, media, newspapers, it's like they teach girls you're supposed to fight. And if anybody had any common sense in their head, they'd know you don't have to fight with the girls in school. . . . Like I mean, you watch TV, you watch MTV, you watch anything, and there's always a fight going on between the popular girls at school. A lot of it is, I mean, you get into a fight and the whole school knows about it. Therefore your popularity goes up. You become more widely known. You're the girl that's in the fight with the other girl. It's like the attention, whether it's positive or negative. It's a constant competition or race for attention.

Of course, socialization is not a simple process. Girls like Bahtya who have "common sense in their head" meet these messages with a range of questions, responses, and viewpoints. But there is no doubt that the increase in images of girlfighting in media contributes to the normalizing of girl-on-girl violence, as well as to the normalization of the reasons and the social contexts in which girls fight.

Fighting itself is not the problem. One can make a strong case for teaching girls how to box or do karate, not only to protect themselves but so they can experience a full sense of power, physical and mental. Indeed, Simone de Beauvoir (1953), writing over fifty years ago, saw the benefits to fighting that transcended competitive sports, "which means specialization and obedience to artificial rules." Such activity "is by no means the equivalent of a free and habitual resort to force," she argued. Sport "does not provide information on the world and the self as intimately as does a free fight" (p. 330). Iris Marion Young (1979) later argued that the messages girls typically receive about femininity "suppress the body potential of women" and provide "a sense that the body is positioned within invisible spatial barriers." These messages have changed radically, but Young's advice to reimagine "our bodies as strong, active subjects moving out to meet the world's risks and confront the resistances of matter and motion" (quoted in Bartky, 1990, p. 35) is still relevant to girls. Girls who fully inhabit their bodies as subjects rather than objects radically alter their relationship to the public world.

It is this sense of power, this refusal to be reduced to the status of object, this desire to be at the heart of her subjectivity, that so often lies behind both girls' growing participation in sports and an increase in physical girlfighting (Adams, 1999, 2006). The problem is that the fighting that girls see in the media and often enact in their relationships is often about containment of other girls—that is, policing sexual behavior, the contours of romantic relationships and friendships, physical appearance, and attitudes (Brown, 2003)—rather than about their freedom of expression.

Given, however, that masculine ideology is defined in part by antifemininity, whenever girls appropriate discourse (or space) traditionally reserved for boys, it destabilizes the sex/gender system and produces cultural anxiety. That there are so many images of girlfighting in the media may thus explain an upsurge in sexual objectification (for example, the Juggy Squad on Comedy Central's *The Man Show*) feminization (extreme makeover shows like *The Swan*), and heightened masculinity (in video games like *Grand Theft Auto* and increased biceps in GI Joe dolls, for example). It may also explain why powerful women, such as sports stars or the women in a reality show like *Survivor,* are asked to pose in sexually provocative ways in men's magazines. Often physical girlfighting itself works to appease that potential anxiety by reestablishing the "natural order"—femininity as subordinate and masculinity as dominant—by feminizing, trivializing, or eroticizing girls' anger and aggression.

Clearly girls appropriate those parts of masculine ideology—not acting like sissies, being in control, exercising dominance, performing with daring and bravado—that they see in the culture enacted by powerful boys and men. They also see these increasingly enacted by girls (on TV shows like *Buffy the Vampire Slayer, Dark Angel,* and *Alias,* and movies like *Charlie's Angels, Tomb Raider,* and *Kill Bill*). But girls are not boys in drag (except in films like *Mulan* or *She's the Man*), and thus although they appropriate aspects of masculine ideology, they do not own it or occupy it as an identity in the same way that boys do. Indeed, as we have suggested, their appropriation serves to create different feminine ideologies and identities that can both challenge and reproduce girls' subordinate social position in relation to boys.

Conclusion

In this chapter we have argued that the phenomenon of girlfighting among early adolescent girls illustrates the complex interrelationship between personal identity and social identity that is the focus of this volume. Using a sociocultural perspective on identity as mediated action, we have shown how girls appropriate forms of masculine ideology from their sociocultural context (specifically, from contemporary media) and use that ideology to shape and affect their actions and interactions with other girls, particularly forms of verbal and physical aggression and fighting. While girlfighting is obviously not the only way in which girls enact and perform their identities, it does provide, we believe, a particularly useful window on the ways in which the social informs the personal and the personal transforms the social.

This analysis also gives rise to several important implications for those who work with girls and boys in schools and other settings:

- There is widespread concern and anxiety in schools—particularly middle schools—about aggression, bullying, and other forms of physical and psychological violence between and among students. Teachers and those working with girls, in particular, need to understand and appreciate the gendered nature of girlfighting, as well as the degree to which it is a culturally mediated enactment of identity. Any systematic attempt to reduce bullying therefore must deal with the fact that our cultural stories and media images about gender, and particularly about girls' and women's relationships, actually cultivate girlfighting behavior.
- As a result, it is critically important for adults to help girls read and critique the culture in which they live, to understand and challenge or interrupt traditional hegemonic masculine ideology (and traditional hegemonic feminine ideology), as well as to resist racist, classist, and homophobic arrangements and ideologies (for useful tips for parents and teachers, see Brown, 2003, and Ward, 2002).
- Adults working with girls must help girls to build coalition groups and solidarity, particularly during the middle school years (see Brown & Madden, 2006). Such efforts will help interrupt the pressure girls feel to take their oppression out on each other, in the form of girlfighting, aggression, bullying, and other forms of what Paulo Freire (1970) called "horizontal violence," and instead encourage them to form a political resistance to the toxic culture in which they live.

- Finally, it is critically important that adults also work with boys to help them understand and resist the "boy code" and the messages it sends about how "real boys" should behave—toward other boys and toward girls (see Pollack, 1998). This work must also include a conversation about male privilege and how to interrupt it, because male privilege enables boys to act toward girls and women in ways that support female subordination, for example, encouraging sexual objectification and eroticizing or trivializing girls' anger and aggression.

The development of a self-observing ego, one of the hallmarks of early adolescence, is an enormous achievement for a young girl. But this age and this achievement also mark a genuine crisis for girls: a moment of both opportunity and danger (see Erikson, 1950). It opens them to different perspectives, allowing them to be more deeply compassionate and intimate and providing them the capability to be critical consumers. It also allows them to develop a heightened sense of self-awareness—to be attuned to how they appear to others, to see themselves as others see her. The danger arises when girls are pressed to give up their own voices in the service of others or to align with a dominant culture that covers over or renders marginal their cultural values and gendered experiences. This is the particular risk that "fighting like a guy" poses for girls. From our sociocultural perspective, what appears to be an expression and enactment of identity and power, critical components of early adolescence, actually holds the potential for constraining, rather than liberating, girls' development.

References

Aapola, S., Gonick, M., & Harris, A. (2005). *Young femininity: Girlhood, power and social change*. New York: Palgrave Macmillan.

Adams, N. (1999). Fighting to be somebody: Resisting erasure and the discursive practices of female adolescent fighting. *Educational Studies, 30*(2), 115–139.

Adams, N. (2006). Girl power: The discursive practices of female fighters and female cheerleaders. In P. Bettis & N. Adams (Eds.). *Geographies of girlhood: Identities in-between* (pp. 101–113). Mahwah, NJ: Erlbaum.

Bartky, S. (1990). *Femininity and domination*. New York: Routledge.

Blasi, A. (1984). Moral identity: Its role in moral functioning. In W. Kurtines & J. Gewirtz (Eds.), *Morality, moral behavior, and moral development* (pp. 128–139). Hoboken, NJ: Wiley.

Brown, L. M. (1998). *Raising their voices: The politics of girls' anger*. Cambridge, MA: Harvard University Press.

Brown, L. M. (2003). *Girlfighting: Betrayal and rejection among girls*. New York: New York University Press.

Brown, L. M., Chesney-Lind, M., & Stein, N. (2007). Patriarchy matters: Toward a gendered theory of teen violence and victimization. *Violence Against Women: An International and Interdisciplinary Journal, 13,* 1249–1273.

Brown, L. M., & Madden, M. (2006). *From adversaries to allies: A curriculum for change*. Waterville, ME: Hardy Girls Healthy Women.

Bruner, J. (1990). *Acts of meaning*. Cambridge, MA: Harvard University Press.

Butler, J. (1990). *Gender trouble: Feminism and the subversion of identity.* New York: Routledge.
Butler, J. (1991). Decking out: Performing identities. In D. Fuss (Ed.), *Inside/out: Lesbian theories, gay theories* (pp. 13–29). New York: Routledge.
Chesney-Lind, M., & Irwin, K. (2007). *Beyond bad girls.* Mahwah, NJ: Erlbaum.
Connell, R. W. (1987). *Gender and power: Society, the person and sexual politics.* Stanford, CA: Stanford University Press.
Crenshaw, K. (1995). Mapping the margins: Intersectionality, identity politics, and violence against women of color. In K. Crenshaw, N. Gotanda, G. Peller, & K. Thomas (Eds.), *Critical race theory: Key writings that formed the movement.* New York: New Press.
de Beauvoir, S. (1953). *The second sex.* New York: Vintage.
Dellasega, C. (2003). *Girl wars.* New York: Fireside.
Erikson, E. (1950). *Childhood and society.* New York: Norton.
Erikson, E. (1968). *Identity: Youth and crisis.* New York: Norton.
Federal Bureau of Investigation. (1991). *Crime in the United States 1990.* Washington, DC: Government Printing Office.
Federal Bureau of Investigation. (2001). *Crime in the United States 2000.* Washington, DC: Government Printing Office.
Feshbach, N. (2005). Gender and the portrayal of direct and indirect aggression on television. In E. Cole & J. Henderson Daniel (Eds.), *Featuring females.* Washington, DC: American Psychological Association.
Freire, P. (1970). *Pedagogy of the oppressed.* New York: Continuum.
Garbarino, J. (2006). *See Jane hit: Why girls are growing more violent and what we can do about it.* New York: Penguin.
Goffman, I. (1959). *The presentation of self in everyday life.* New York: Doubleday Anchor.
Holland, D., Lachicotte, W., Skinner, D., & Cain, C. (1998). *Identity and agency in cultural worlds.* Cambridge, MA: Harvard University Press.
Lamb, S., & Brown, L. M. (2006). *Packaging girlhood: Rescuing our daughters from marketers' schemes.* New York: St. Martin's Press.
Meadows, S., & D. Johnson. (2003, May 19). Girl fight: Savagery in the Chicago suburbs. *Newsweek, 37.*
Penuel, W., & Wertsch, J. (1995). Vygotsky and identity formation: A sociocultural approach. *Educational Psychologist, 30,* 83–92.
Pleck, J., Sonenstein, F., & Ku, L. (1993). Masculinity ideology and its correlates. In S. Oskamp & M. Costanzo (Eds.), *Gender issues in contemporary society* (pp. 85–110). Thousand Oaks, CA: Sage.
Pollack, W. (1998). *Real boys: Rescuing our sons from the myths of boyhood.* New York: Holt.
Prothrow-Stith, D., Spivak, H., & Reno, J. (2006). *Sugar and spice and no longer nice.* San Francisco: Jossey-Bass.
Rogoff, B. (1995). Observing sociocultural activity on three planes: Participatory appropriation, guided participation, and apprenticeship. In J. Wertsch, P. del Rio, & A. Alvarez (Eds.), *Sociocultural studies of mind* (pp. 139–164). Cambridge: Cambridge University Press.
Simmons, R. (2002). *Odd girl out.* New York: Harcourt.
Talbot, M. (2002, February 24). Girls just want to be mean. *New York Times Magazine,* 24–64.
Tappan, M. (2000). Autobiography, mediated action, and the development of moral identity. *Narrative Inquiry, 10,* 81–109.
Tappan, M. (2001). The cultural reproduction of masculinity: A critical perspective on boys' development. In M. Packer & M. Tappan (Eds.), *Cultural and critical perspectives on human development.* Albany: State University of New York Press.
Tappan, M. (2005). Domination, subordination, and the dialogical self: Identity development and the politics of "ideological becoming." *Culture and Psychology, 11*(1), 47–75.

Vygotsky, L. (1978). *Mind in society: The development of higher psychological processes* (M. Cole, V. John-Steiner, S. Scribner, & E. Souberman, Eds.). Cambridge, MA: Harvard University Press.

Ward, J. (2002). *The skin we're in: Teaching our teens to be emotionally strong, socially smart, and spiritually connected.* New York: Free Press.

Wertsch, J. (1998). *Mind as action.* New York: Oxford University Press.

Wiseman, R. (2003). *Queen bees and wannabees.* New York: Crown.

Young, I. M. (1979, September). *Is there a woman's world? Some reflections on the struggle for our bodies.* Lecture presented to the Second Sex—Thirty Years Later: A Commemorative Conference on Feminist Theory, New York Institute for the Humanities, New York University, New York.

LYN MIKEL BROWN is a professor of education at Colby College in Waterville, Maine.

MARK B. TAPPAN is a professor of education and human development at Colby College in Waterville, Maine.

Way, N., Santos, C., Niwa, E. Y., & Kim-Gervey, C. (2008). To be or not to be: An exploration of ethnic identity development in context. In M. Azmitia, M. Syed, & K. Radmacher (Eds.), *The intersections of personal and social identities. New Directions for Child
and Adolescent Development, 120*, 61–79.

To Be or Not to Be: An Exploration of Ethnic Identity Development in Context

*Niobe Way, Carlos Santos, Erika Y. Niwa,
Constance Kim-Gervey*

Abstract

*This qualitative study focused on the intersection of personal and ethnic identi-
ties among forty African American, Puerto Rican, Dominican, and Chinese
American high school students. The patterns in content indicated that for the
Puerto Ricans, the intersection of their personal and social identities was a series
of accommodations to a positive peer climate and a resistance to being Dominican. For the other ethnic groups, the intersection of their personal and social
identities consisted of a process of resistance and accommodation to negative
stereotypes projected on them by their peers and, for African Americans, themselves.* © Wiley Periodicals, Inc.

All students' names in the chapter have been changed to protect their privacy.

W ith the dramatic increase in the ethnic diversity of the United States (Portes & Rumbaut, 2001), we have seen a corresponding increase in the number of studies focused on ethnic identity and the ways in which ethnic identity is linked to psychological and social adjustment (Phinney, 1990; Yip, Seaton, & Sellers, 2006). A strong attachment to one's own ethnic group, the most common definition of ethnic identity, has been shown to correlate significantly with high self-esteem, low levels of depressive symptoms, good grades, high-quality friendships, and numerous other indicators of adjustment in cross-sectional and longitudinal studies of adolescents. Despite this growing body of research on ethnic identity, there remain fundamental gaps in our understanding of this critical aspect of social identity. Most striking, we know little about the lived or personal experience of ethnicity, or how "individuals come to develop a personal understanding of their own social identities" (see Chapter One, this volume). What is the meaning for the individual of being attached to his or her ethnic group? How does the context shape his or her attachment to his or her ethnic/racial group?

The assumption implicit in most studies of ethnic identity is that the processes by which ethnic identity is experienced, interpreted, and enacted is similar across contexts or settings. Although ecological models of development (Bronfenbrenner, 1979) have encouraged a generation of psychologists to understand developmental processes in context, the study of ethnic identity continues to be analyzed, for the most part, with little sensitivity to the contexts of these identities. Contexts may influence not only the levels of ethnic pride but also the meaning of social identities.

The purpose of the present study was to use semistructured interviews to explore African American, Puerto Rican, Dominican, and Chinese American adolescents' experiences of their own ethnicity or ethnic identity and how the contexts in which the adolescents are embedded shape such experiences. Our goal is to reveal how personal and social identities are woven together and are part of a political, economic, and social context (see Cooper, 1999).

Ethnic Identity

The most common definition of ethnic identity draws from social psychology (Tajfel, 1978) and indicates that ethnic identity entails, for the most part, a sense of belonging or attachment to one's own ethnic group (Phinney, 1990; Phinney & Rotheram, 1987). Although research on ethnic identity has offered critical insights into the correlates of ethnic identity, it has been limited methodologically and conceptually. Standardized surveys, for example, have been the primary form of data collection and have assessed different dimensions of ethnic identity (for example, sense of attachment) within and across ethnic groups and the ways in which such dimensions correlate with outcomes such as psychological adjustment. Yet classic studies of boys' (see Erikson, 1968) and girls' (see Brown & Gilligan, 1992; Chapter Four, this volume) identity development have repeatedly underscored the nuanced and complex nature of identity development and called for, implicitly and explicitly, more qualitative studies in which the meaning and the political and social contexts that shape that meaning are explored. Conceptualizing ethnic or any other social identity as exclusively a study of the extent to which (or "level") a person feels proud of, attached to, or positive about his or her ethnic group misses a large part of the process of identity development—a process that, according to over three decades of work, entails constant negotiation, renegotiation, resistance, and accommodation (Erikson, 1968; Brown & Gilligan, 1992).

The few researchers who have examined the experience of ethnicity or ethnic identity using qualitative methods have found that the ways in which ethnicity is experienced varies by the contexts in which such identities are constructed (Torres & Magolda, 2004; Phinney & Tarver, 1988). Wilkins (2004), for example, interviewed "Puerto Rican wannabees," White middle-class girls who had been labeled by their White, Black, and Puerto Rican peers as "wannabees" due to their adherence to stereotypical ideas of toughness and sexuality associated with Puerto Rican culture and to the fact that they dated Puerto Rican and Black men. Her study revealed how social identities are interwoven and constantly being redefined by the acceptance and rejection of others within and outside one's own social group. Niemann, Romero, Arredondo, and Rodriguez's (1999) research on Mexican American college students also draws attention to the ways in which the experience of one's own ethnicity is bounded by the perceptions of and interactions with other ethnic groups, including those who are in the majority as well as those who are in the minority (Niemann et al., 1999; Rumbaut, 2005; Rosenbloom & Way; 2004; Qin & Way, in press)

This small body of qualitative work, however, has focused primarily on young adults or college students and White and Black young people. Adolescence, however, is also a critical period for identity development (Erikson, 1968), as this is the period in which young people often have the safety network of their families to explore and construct their identities. In addition, adolescents live in an increasingly multiethnic world where the development of identity is no longer a Black and White issue. Examining how adolescents of color, including Puerto Rican, Dominican, African American, and Chinese American adolescents, experience their personal and social identities in the context of a multiethnic community is critical to advancing our understanding of ethnic identity development.

Ethnic Identity in Context

Ecological models of development indicate that children and adolescents exist within multiple intersecting and overlapping proximal (peers, family, and school) and distal (the social, economic, and political climate) contexts

NEW DIRECTIONS FOR CHILD AND ADOLESCENT DEVELOPMENT • DOI: 10.1002/cd

and that these multiple ecological systems in large part determine the course of adolescent development (Bronfenbrenner, 1979; Cooper 1999). Consequently, the child who is at the core of the ecological system and the contexts in which she or he is embedded should not be considered in isolation from one another but rather viewed as a web of interacting systems.

This framework suggests that adolescents' perceptions of their ethnicity and ethnic groups are influenced by multiple layers of a dynamic ecological system, including families, schools, and peers, as well as the political, social, and economic climate. Drawing from such ecological theories of development, researchers have increasingly examined the ways in which the family shapes various dimensions of ethnic identity among adolescents (French, Seidman, Allen, & Aber, 2000; Umana-Taylor, 2004). Fewer studies, however, have looked beyond the family to include proximal contexts such as schools as a context of identity development. And those who have studied school contexts have focused exclusively on the extent to which the proportion of different ethnic/racial groups within the school influences adolescents' ethnic identities (French et al., 2000; Umana-Taylor, 2003). Yet there are multiple ways in which schools may influence ethnic identity, including the quality of relationships among students and teachers and the social hierarchy of the students within the school (Way, Kim, & Santos, 2005; Wilkins, 2004). Qualitative research suggests that ethnic/racial discrimination by teachers and students, for example, has a critical influence on the ways in which adolescents experience their personal and social identities (Rosenbloom & Way, 2004; Rumbaut, 2005; Verkuyten, 2005). In addition to the school, there is also the larger sociopolitical environment in which schools exist. While much theoretical work has been done exploring how these more macrocontexts shape child development (see Tamis-Lemonda, Way, Yoshikawa, Hughes, & Niwa, 2008), few scholars have explored how these larger contexts shape the experience of identity in particular.

To address these large gaps in the literature on ethnic identity, our study sought to explore (1) the experience of ethnicity and ethnic identity among primarily low-income African American, Puerto Rican, Dominican, and Chinese American adolescents from New York City; (2) how experiences of ethnicity and ethnic identity differed across ethnic groups; and (3) how the context of school, particularly the relationships within the school, and the larger context of New York City shaped the experiences of ethnicity and ethnic identity.

Method

To contextualize the adolescents' construction of ethnicity and ethnic identity, we first describe the characteristics of the high schools they attended and the ways in which we gathered our data. Describing the context is a critical component of qualitative approach for our study.

NEW DIRECTIONS FOR CHILD AND ADOLESCENT DEVELOPMENT • DOI: 10.1002/cd

Context. Students were drawn from two urban public high schools located in the same neighborhood in New York City. Most students in the two schools were eligible for federal assistance through the free lunch program (over 80 percent in each school), and both schools were racially and ethnically diverse (40 to 45 percent Latino, mostly Puerto Rican and Dominican; 30 to 34 percent Asian American, mostly Chinese American; and 14 to 18 percent African American). Both schools had only 1 to 2 percent White students (primarily eastern European). These schools were highly segregated as determined by who was sitting together in the lunchroom; the Chinese students were the most segregated. In both schools, the teachers were almost exclusively White (except in bilingual classes). The students attending both schools were mostly from the neighborhood, except the African American students, who often commuted to one of the two schools (approximately a thirty- to sixty-minute commute) because of its reputation of being a safe school (neither of them had metal detectors in the entrance to the school).

Our participant observation and interviews in these two schools over the course of four years consistently indicated that the social hierarchy among the students was a core context for identity development. While the Puerto Ricans represented approximately only 25 percent of the students in either school, they were consistently considered the "coolest" students by their peers. Conversations in the lunchroom and hallways indicated that they were on the top of the peer social hierarchy because of their "attitude" (assertive and confident), music, style, and, last but certainly not the least important in the eyes of most of the students, the Puerto Rican girls had the "best hair" and they, along with the Puerto Rican boys, had fair skin but were not White. None of the students wanted to be White, which was equated with being the oppressor. However, the students' idealization of the Puerto Rican students, students who in skin color and hair texture were most like White students but were not White, suggested that race and racism infused the peer social hierarchy. Finally, the Puerto Rican students were admired because they were not immigrants.

The Chinese American students, who were numerically better represented than the Puerto Ricans (approximately 30 percent) but were from predominantly immigrant families who did not speak English, were on the bottom of the peer social hierarchy. They were considered by non-Chinese students as "dirty," "smelly," and "not cool" in personal style, food habits, language, and general attitudes. The African Americans, who were the clear ethnic minority in both schools (14 to 18 percent), had more social capital than their Chinese American peers due to their hip-hop clothing style, music, language, and attitude. However, they did not share the same level of social clout as their Puerto Rican peers. Finally the Dominicans were more accepted than the Chinese Americans by other students because they were considered "Latino" like the Puerto Ricans, but due to their immigrant status and darker skin color, they too were often disparaged as old-fashioned and "not cool."

Participants

In both schools, 167 participants were interviewed once each year for at least three years. From this larger sample, we purposively selected 40 students (10 in each ethnic group) based on seeking equal numbers of males and females in each race/ethnic category. Forty percent of our sample were from single-parent homes, and 20 percent were first-generation immigrants.

Procedure

Qualitative data were collected during the fall semesters of 1996, 1997, 1998, and 1999 in school 1 and fall semesters of 1999, 2000, 2001, and 2002 in school 2. During the first year of the study in each school, students were recruited from mainstream English classes to ensure that study participants were at least somewhat fluent English speakers because the interviews were conducted in English. Approximately 85 percent of the students within each school attended mainstream English classes. The interviews were held during the school day, lasted approximately ninety minutes, and took place in an office in which confidentiality could be assured. The interviews were conducted each year by an ethnically diverse group of graduate students in psychology who had been extensively trained in interviewing techniques by the first author. All interviews were audiotaped and transcribed for analysis.

Interviews. All students participated in a series of three or four one-to-one semistructured interviews (one each year for four years) in which they were asked to discuss their attitudes and beliefs about their own ethnic group. The interview protocol included questions such as: "How would you describe your ethnic group?" and "What does being . . . . mean to you?" Although each interview included a standard set of questions, follow-up questions varied across interviews to capture the adolescents' own ways of describing their ethnicity and ethnic group.

Participant Observation. The interviewers also conducted participant observation in both schools during the first two years of each study. The participant observation entailed at least one member of the team visiting the school each week and observing hallways, lunchrooms, extracurricular activities, and classrooms. These observations included attending evening events organized by the school. In addition, interviewers and participant observers offered various forms of assistance, such as creative workshops, to teachers and students. These activities allowed the participant observers to become "active members" in the school environment (Adler & Adler, 1987). Following Lofland and Lofland (1995), they obtained "intimate familiarity" and the "richest possible data" in a naturalistic setting. The notes from the participant observations provided contextual information that aided in the interpretations of the interview data offered in this paper (see Way, 1998).

Data Analysis. We used a process of open coding (see Strauss & Corbin, 1990) to generate themes from the interview data. We (the chapter authors) first read through the forty interviews and created narrative summaries that condensed the interview material while retaining the essence of the stories told by the adolescents (see Miller, 1991). We read each narrative summary independently, looking for themes in the summaries. In any one year of the study, a theme retained for further analysis had to be identified as a theme independently by at least two of the data analysts. Once themes were generated and agreed on, each data analyst returned to the original interviews and noted the year in the project and the specific place in the interview where these themes emerged. They also took note of if and how the themes changed during the four years of the study.

Findings

We detected patterns in both the form and content of the narratives over the four years of the study. The primary pattern in form was the form of students' responses to our questions about ethnicity. When we asked them about their ethnicity, they spoke about (1) who they were, (2) who they wanted to be, and (3) who they did not want to be. This pattern fits closely with Erikson's idea (1968) that identity development is not only a process of what one wants to be but also of who one does not want to be. Many of the students' interviews were in fact dominated by discussions of who they did not want to be. As we listened to Puerto Rican, Dominican, African American, and Chinese American adolescents speak about who they are, who they want to be, and who they do not want to be, we saw their identity struggles come to the fore and gained a deeper understanding of the intersection of their personal and social identities and how the proximal and distal contexts in which they are embedded shape these processes.

Puerto Rican Students.

Who Am I? and Who Do I Want To Be? "Puerto Rican!" Jorge, a Puerto Rican teenager, stated, "To me, [being Puerto Rican] means having a rich culture. 'Cause I have gone around Puerto Rico and seen how rich the culture is. How refined it is now." Juan viewed his Puerto Rican heritage positively: "[I am] always proud to say, 'Oh, I'm Puerto Rican!'" When we asked Juan why he was proud of being Puerto Rican, he stated that "it's just like a natural sense that oh, I'm Puerto Rican, I'm damn proud of it. So I don't really know why I'm proud of it, but I know I am." Immersed in a positive social climate, the Puerto Rican students sounded confident about and proud of their Puerto Rican community during each year of the study. The Puerto Rican pride, which permeated the entire school context, fostered a sense of pride, like Juan's, that was rooted not in a concrete fact or experience but simply in being Puerto Rican.

NEW DIRECTIONS FOR CHILD AND ADOLESCENT DEVELOPMENT • DOI: 10.1002/cd

Some students, however, had reasons for their pride and those reasons included having an idealized image of the island of Puerto Rico. "It's a nice place," Arnaldo said, "I mean Puerto Rico's real nice. No [I haven't been there] but I've seen pictures and everything like that and it shows." Similarly, when we asked Ricardo what being Puerto Rican meant to him, he stated that "it's good, um, I'm happy being Puerto Rican. . . . I come from a beautiful place, you know, the culture is beautiful and you never get beautiful here." The contrast between "here" and Puerto Rico was an important component of the students' sense of being Puerto Rican.

The Puerto Rican students were also proud of the accomplishments of their community. Hector said: "I think being Puerto Rican is good because like a lot of Puerto Ricans are achieving more than what they used to. And they are doing more things and learning more things. . . . Like they're trying to achieve more from what they used to."

The Puerto Rican students' pride was focused on the present moment— what Puerto Rico looked like and what Puerto Ricans were doing now. This focus seemed to reflect, at least in part, their apparent lack of knowledge regarding Puerto Rican history, a history that was not incorporated into the curriculum in their schools. None of the Puerto Rican students brought up Puerto Rican history when discussing their ethnicity or ethnic group.

The students' sense of pride was also based on the Puerto Rican Day Parade, an annual New York City event. In response to what it meant to him to be Puerto Rican, Alberto said: "That I'm proud, and I'm happy that I'm in that culture." And in response to, "Okay, what are you proud of? Is there any specific things?" he replied, "That my culture is real strong and loving. "And when asked, "How is it strong and loving?" he responded, 'Cause we got a lot of respect for each other and we like to get together all the time like the Puerto Rican Parade. There is a lot of love there."

Repeatedly over the course of the study, the Puerto Rican students referred to the Puerto Rican Parade as a critical part of their experience of being Puerto Rican. This parade is one of the few citywide celebrations that take place on Fifth Avenue, the main artery that runs through New York City. City officials no longer issue permits for parades at this location because of its centrality and its effect on the traffic flow of the city. The fact that this event still takes place on Fifth Avenue each year speaks to the political and social clout that the Puerto Rican community has in New York City life.

The role of the Puerto Rican Parade on the identities of the students underscores the ways in which the political and social context of New York City influences social and personal identities. The parade was even used as a source of contrast to distinguish what it meant to be Puerto Rican versus being Dominican. Jasmine, whose mother is Dominican and father is Puerto Rican and who identifies with being Puerto Rican, said:

> Well I think the Puerto Ricans are, well not stronger, but they're more like, hey this is what I am, I'm proud. 'Cause when I went to the Puerto Rican parade

with my dad and my uncles and stuff, they're like very yeah! And all these flags and all this drama. But then like when I went to the Dominican parade with my mom and my grandma and stuff, they're like wave the flag and watch the things go by. And I'm like whoa, it's so different. It's like, I can't explain it. It's like, Puerto Ricans, like, are more loud. I don't know. More crazy.

Jasmine's narrative draws attention to the ways in which adolescents' experiences of their ethnic identities are bound to the structural, social, and political opportunities within particular contexts.

Who Do I Not Want to Be? "Don't Call Me Dominican!" Laura, a Puerto Rican, said of other Puerto Rican students, 'They always say: Oh, I'm not Dominican, don't call me Dominican . . . They [Dominicans] have a lot of the same things, but they also have a lot of different things. Dominicans have lots of words in their language that's different than ours. They eat a lot of different foods and stuff. And they're darker and stuff like that."

Like the reasons for preferring the Puerto Rican students, the reasons for not wanting to be Dominican reveal the political and social structure in which skin color matters. When Yadira was asked about how being Puerto Rican affects her friendships, she too revealed the power structure that embeds the adolescents' identities:

One time right like there was this girl named Jackie, she is Dominican and you know how they always saying that Dominicans are immigrants. So one day in Spanish class the teacher said that all the Dominicans in the class have to do something. And Jackie was in the class and she's like come with me, come with me. And I said "Jackie I'm not coming with you, 'cause you're still an immigrant." And um she got all mad and there was a whole big fight because of that, forget it. . . . We just stopped talking.

Characterizations of the Dominican students by the Puerto Ricans as "immigrants" or "darker" support ecological theories of identity development (Erikson, 1968; Cooper, 1999; Rumbaut, 2005) that argue that identities, including what one does not want to be as well as what one wants to be, are products of the political and social context in which identities are constructed. It is only, however, when the Puerto Ricans discuss who they do not want to be that the social and political structure becomes readily apparent. Puerto Ricans, who have more social clout than their Black and Dominican peers in the school but remain an ethnic minority in a city and country dominated by White European American people, do not want to be confused with their Latino cousins who are not only darker but are not American. The Puerto Rican students underscore the demarcations of skin tone and citizenship status to help foster their sense of power in a context in which they do not share real power outside their school but have more social power within the school than most of the other students.

Dominican Students.

Who Am I? "Dominican." Rivaldo, a Dominican teenager, noted how being Dominican affects his friendships: "I mean my friends [who are Puerto Rican] will joke around with me and call me 'dumb in a can.' Why? 'Cause it's like Dominican . . . he's like 'DUM–I N–A–CAN.'" Edwin, a Dominican teenager, said, "Well, sometimes [the Puerto Ricans] joke around and call me 'Platano' [*plantain*], but that's joking around. . . . I take no offense."

Immersed in a negative peer context, the Dominican students often voiced ambivalence about being Dominican. Sometimes the ambivalence was obvious: Sergio said in the same breath about his Dominican culture: "I love it. . . . It's not that important to me." Other times the ambivalence was more subtle. José had this to say when asked how he felt about being Dominican: "Yeah, I mean, I'm proud of it. I really don't, like, show it much but yeah, I am." The interviewer then asked, "What are you proud of?" and José responded, "I'm proud of being Dominican. Some people like my sister, she doesn't like it. But I am what I am and I can't change it, so I gotta stay there." When asked why his sister does not like being Dominican, he explained: "'Cause all her friends are Puerto Ricans. So she's young so she really don't understand it. All her friends are Puerto Rican so that's what she wants to be too." His transition from being "proud to be Dominican" to confessing that his sister would rather be Puerto Rican suggests that he too, like his sister, is ambivalent about being Dominican. The struggle for the Dominican students was to remain proud in a hostile Puerto Rican peer context.

Who Do I Want to Be? "Puerto Rican." Sergio, a Dominican young man, described the tensions between Dominicans and Puerto Ricans:

> It's just where you come from. Like they always arguing outside about Puerto Rican, Dominican, I say 'yo what's the difference, brother!' You were born on top of a table or a hospital or in a car or not. It's no difference, it's just where you were born at.

> This bunch of guys outside yesterday [was arguing this]. I was like, what's the difference? They told my man George was like "Oh, the Puerto Rican parade is longer than the Dominican parade. And I was like, "what's the big deal." Oh my god, when they argue they go on for hours and hours. I just be sitting there, I be like shut up. . . . I don't know 'cause I ain't gonna lie. A lot of Dominicans act like teenagers and stuff. They act up too much. Like they don't know how to act. . . . Like I don't like chilling with them a lot, and that's my culture. You know, I hardly hang out with a lot of Dominicans 'cause I can't, they don't know how to act. . . . They act like they never seen a girl before like I'm not gonna lie. They seen my sister and they stare her down and I get mad. . . . I hate that.

Sergio's story, which entails moving from resisting negative stereotypes of his ethnic group to accommodating to those very same stereotypes, suggests that he desires both to be and not to be Dominican. Students' frustration with being Dominican often came on the heels of claiming to be unclear about why there was so much tension between Puerto Ricans and Dominicans. Diana, a half-Dominican and half–Puerto Rican teenager, spoke of what it means to be both ethnicities: "It's hard, it's very hard because like you know how the whole—it's not a war, but it's Dominican versus Puerto Ricans and the whole thing." Like the girls in Brown and Gilligan's studies (1992), the Dominican students stated that they did not know why there was tension and then proceeded to explain why there was this "war" (for example, because "Dominicans don't know how to act properly"). Although none of the Dominican students explicitly indicated that they wanted to be Puerto Rican, their comments about other Dominicans wanting to be Puerto Rican and their frustrations with being Dominican in contrast to Puerto Rican suggested a desire to be identified with the higher-status group.

Who Do I Not Want to Be? "Dominican." Throughout the four years of the study, the Dominican students struggled with issues of skin color, citizenship status, and negative stereotypes about their language, culture, and food. Although they never indicated explicitly that they did not want to be Dominican, their stories suggested that they were not at home in their skin literally and metaphorically. Christina said about the stereotypes of Dominicans, "You always think like we're always dark-skinned. Like everyone's like has dark skin, black hair, black eyes. Like my cousin Jennifer, she's like, not dark. She has blonde hair, blonde, blonde hair, and like really, like bluish-green eyes, and she's very, very light. . . . So not everybody is like, dark skinned."

The Dominican students' experience of ethnicity was woven tightly together with experiences of race and racism. They were constantly in the process of resisting what others (primarily Puerto Ricans) projected onto them. This stance of constant vigilance and resistance, as well as accommodation, to the stereotypes suggests that both the form and content of the experience of personal and social identity are distinct from those of the Puerto Rican students. While the Puerto Ricans accommodate to the idealized notions of being Puerto Rican perpetuated by students in the school, the Dominicans both resist and accommodate to their peers' projections.

African American Students.
Who am I? "African American." While the Dominicans were immersed in a negative peer climate, the African American students were immersed in a negative adult climate perpetuated predominantly by White teachers, store owners, and police in the city. Robert told his interviewer:

> Um, I was on my way to a party, me, my cousin, and couple of other friends, police jumped out the car, pulled out their guns on us, slammed us into doors cursing at us, they like everything ask—after everything was over we ask officer what was the problem. We looked like possible suspects. Wow, all ten of us? And they just kept kept saying, 'get the hell out of here—niggers.'

NEW DIRECTIONS FOR CHILD AND ADOLESCENT DEVELOPMENT • DOI: 10.1002/cd

In seeming response to these negative experiences, the African American students' discussion of their ethnic/racial identity emphasized the history and the pride that grew out of the opposition to racism in their communities. When Robert was asked why being African American was important to him, he said

> Yeah it's important. . . . The way we came up. As an ethnic group. We had people like Martin Luther King and Malcolm X, Marcus Garvey. People who fought for us to come up to where we are now. That's important to me because I'm African American too and as they helped me come up as a person, that builds my self-confidence and to let me know that I could be anything that I want to be and do anything I want to do.

Unlike the other students, the African American students consistently drew from their own histories to build a sense of pride, although at times they questioned the relevance of this history to their own personal identities. The African Americans students' focus on the past likely stems from the inclusion of Black history in high school history curriculums and small parts of mainstream culture. While the Puerto Ricans and Dominicans are learning about their cultures through the Puerto Rican or Dominican parade—a celebration of food, people, culture, and place—and through visiting their islands, the African American students are learning about their culture (at least the history of slavery and civil rights) through history class and Black History Month. Their stories implicitly underscore the importance of exploring the source of knowledge in studies of identity development.

Who Do I Want to Be? "A Role Model." The desire of the African American students was not to be from another ethnic group but to be a role model within their own community. And wanting to be a role model was intimately linked to wanting to challenge negative stereotypes of African American people. Kim noted the importance of being a positive Black role model by doing well in school:

> Because there's a lot of positive Black people, like that have education and stuff like that, so I know that I can do it too. It's not like nobody or no Black person ever went to college before, you know there's people that have gone before and are still going, so like they've done it, and I know I can do it too basically. So it's a positive influence.

Kim noted her own desire to achieve and become a positive role model as contingent on the existence of other positive Black role models. While she hinted at prevailing negative stereotypes about the academic success of African Americans, some students were more explicit about the need to actively resist such negative stereotypes by embodying positive pathways as role models.

NEW DIRECTIONS FOR CHILD AND ADOLESCENT DEVELOPMENT • DOI: 10.1002/cd

The desire to be positive role models was also laced with a desire to transcend their race and become raceless, a desire that reflects the insidious ways that racist stereotypes function in the identity development of youth. If they cannot challenge the negative stereotypes, the alternative, the students implicitly suggested, is not to have a race. When asked to describe themselves, the African American students often focused on "being human." For Karen, fitting into a racial category was both "what it is" and something to transcend: "When they asked me what race I am, I say I'm human, but, you know, I'm a say it because some kids lie about what they are. If you're Black, you're Black, if you're White you're White, it doesn't matter . . . whatever comes out the most is what you are." In response to how "some kids lie" about their race, she noted the importance of both identifying yourself racially and seeing yourself as transcending those categories.

When asked to describe what being Black meant to her, Sarah responded:

> It doesn't really mean nothing to me, it's just being like the color of your skin. To me . . . it's not really, it doesn't matter like what color I am, I still be important, like it doesn't even matter, 'cause people expect us to be like you know stupid or whatever. It's hard. Yeah, some people teachers be like, in my school, we got some racist teachers.

In Sarah's struggle to transcend race, she reiterated the racist beliefs that led her to desire such transcendence. Ironically the strategy that she used to challenge racist stereotypes underscores the relevance of race and racism in her personal and social identities and those of her African American peers. The desire to transcend race was clearly a response to an environment in which talking about race is greatly discouraged and where Puerto Ricans have such high peer status because, in part, they do not "look Black."

Who Do I Not Want to Be? "A Stereotype." Similar to their discussion of what they wanted to be, the African American students did not use another ethnic/racial group as the foil against which they built their sense of identity (see also Phinney & Tarver, 1988); rather, they used the negative stereotypes about their culture as their foil. They did not want to be a stereotype, whether that was a drug addict, a teenage mother, a dropout, or a gang member. Lisa argued:

> Like 'cause most of crime population and the drugs populations, who buys what? Black people. . . . And so, like, that's what makes people bad, because other Black people don't think. You have to think. I mean, thinking is important. I'm just saying, you know, you should think. And it's like that, that, that just—that makes us look bad. It's like, "Why are you doing this?" You don't think about other people? I mean, you should think about yourself, but you should think about other people also.

NEW DIRECTIONS FOR CHILD AND ADOLESCENT DEVELOPMENT • DOI: 10.1002/cd

Lisa described the need for others within her own community to resist negative behavior. The fact that the out-group against which the African American students distinguished themselves were the people within their own community who perpetuated negative stereotypes as well as the stereotypes themselves suggests that the process of identity formation for these students entails both resistance—a resistance to stereotypes—and accommodation to those very same stereotypes in their refusal at times to be identified as Black.

Chinese American Students.

Who Am I? "A Victim of Harassment." Michael, a Chinese American adolescent, said that being Chinese meant, "In general, I would say, [sharp inhale and exhale] you get discriminated against. . . . Sometimes." Another student described being Chinese as "the weak race." Due to their immigrant status, their accents, their relatively small physical size, especially among the boys, and the preference the teachers had for most Asian students (see Rosenbloom & Way, 2004), the Chinese American students were the most likely to be disliked, harassed, yelled at, hit, and generally victimized by their non-Chinese peers. Although the Dominican students in this sample were also teased for being immigrants, their similarities to the Puerto Ricans in the outward markers of their ethnicity such as language helped to counteract such victimization.

Such victimization ranged from verbal harassment and name-calling, to having things thrown at them by non-Chinese students, to being physically assaulted. Students experienced being called names that were specifically related to their ethnicity, such as "chink" and "chino," and to other slurs such as "nerd" and "shorty." Victimization both inside and outside school was linked to language skills and to immigrant status (see Qin & Way, in press). One student said, "[The people in this school] hate the Chinese because when [the Chinese] speak Chinese, these people don't understand so they slap the face of the Chinese person who is talking."

Chinese students often tried to justify the extent of peer harassment they experienced. When asked about discrimination, Phoebe responded, "Usually Chinese people don't fight back. That's the culture too. That's why people keep picking on Chinese because they just don't stick together. They just say 'oh like, I gonna go.' I mean if like, if one Chinese person gets beat up, the other Chinese people around them won't help out. They just watch it happen, and let it happen." Qing said, "Basically they pick on Chinese people 'cause Chinese are not as united as, you know, others. They don't get close to each other when there's a problem so people like to pick on the Chinese. . . . Us Chinese are not united enough." Although some of the Chinese youth attributed their lack of response to "culture," such a response was likely due to their fear that they would be picked on too if they helped defend a friend.

Other Chinese students thought the problem was that the Chinese were too smart for their own good. Said Jian Hong, "And all American people think all Chinese people are smart, so they always bother Chinese people, always call them Chinos and stuff. . . . Black people, people from other countries who live here . . . they think that Chinese are, like, all weak, and that these Americans should beat the Chinese up, that's why they bother them." The insidious racism produced responses such as these that blame victims of racism for the ways in which they are treated.

Who Do I Want to Be? "Puerto Rican or Black." Alice said, "I don't like to be Chinese." When asked why, she responded, "I don't know why. I just feel like I want to be Puerto Rican or something." Students, particularly American-born Chinese, expressed a desire to be Puerto Rican or Black by dressing like and aligning themselves with Puerto Rican and Black youth. Like the peers of the "Puerto Rican Wannabees" whom Wilkins (2004) describes in her study, many of the Chinese immigrant peers expressed irritation at the extent to which American-born Chinese tried to act as if they were Puerto Rican or Black. Tony said to his interviewer: "If you went to some of the . . . asked them [the American-born Chinese], what are your race? They would say I'm Black, but they're actually Chinese." The desire to be Puerto Rican or Black revealed both a resistance to static ethnic categories but also an accommodation to the larger peer context in which all the students, with the exception of the African American students, wanted to be Puerto Rican.

Who Do I Not Want to Be? "Chinese." Russel said, "At times I wish I wasn't Chinese 'cause people insult me." Another student also lamented being Chinese: "I really hate other kids pick on us Chinese. That's why sometimes I don't like being Chinese 'cause they're small. I wish I was huge. Yeah, I wish I could, like I always hated being small. Always hated it. Other people are so big and I'm just skinny." While many Chinese American students directly expressed the desire not to be Chinese, other students simply distanced themselves from their Chinese peers as a way "not to be" Chinese. Grace, a young Chinese adolescent, said, "I just cannot be with Chinese people, like friends, I can't be with them. It's hard 'cause I don't feel like Chinese people. I don't feel like being with Chinese people. I feel like being with these [non-Chinese] people now, like in the hallways, with walking around with those people, I feel good with those people."

Like the Puerto Ricans, the Chinese American students' identity development appears to be a process of accommodation to the social hierarchy within the school. However, their status on the social hierarchy is on the opposite end of the scale from the Puerto Ricans, and thus the process of accommodation does not entail a process of pride and self-love but a process of negation and self-hate. While there were occasional signs of resistance to these negative stereotypes, the overwhelming theme for the Chinese American students was one of accommodation to these stereotypes.

NEW DIRECTIONS FOR CHILD AND ADOLESCENT DEVELOPMENT • DOI: 10.1002/cd

Discussion

Our analysis revealed patterns in both the form and content of adolescents' experiences of ethnicity and ethnic identity development. The patterns in form underscored the ways in which ethnic identity development is a process of constructing—in relation to one's ethnic group—who one is, who one wants to be or is becoming, as well as who one does not want to be. At times the interviews of the students suggested that the experiences of ethnicity and ethnic identity are more entangled with what "haunts you at night" (Erikson, 1968, p. 22) or the person one most resists becoming (for example, a negative stereotype) than with who one is or wants to be. For some, in fact, who one *is* seemed to be mostly, if not fully, about who one is *not*.

The interviews revealed the ways in which personal and social identities intersect and the ways in which these identities are a product of the social and political context. For the Puerto Ricans, the intersection of personal and social identities—who they are with what their ethnic group or social group is—was a series of accommodations to a generally positive peer climate and a resistance to being Dominican. The foil against which they developed their identities was the Dominican youth to whom they regularly distinguished themselves and to whom they considered themselves superior. Their sense of themselves— their personal identities—was strongly linked to being Puerto Rican, and that experience of being Puerto Rican was strongly linked to not being Dominican.

For the Dominicans, the intersection of their identities consisted of a process of resistance and accommodation to the negative stereotypes projected on them by their Puerto Rican peers primarily. Their sense of themselves was strongly linked to being Dominican, but the experience of being Dominican was riddled with ambivalence as they both experienced pride in their ethnic group and shame and frustration.

For the African American youth, the development of their identities also consisted of a process of resistance and accommodation, but their resistance was not group specific as it was for the Dominicans. Rather, the foil against which they constructed their identities was the negative stereotypes projected onto them by all ethnic groups, including their own. These youth seemed to struggle at times to connect their personal and social identities for fear, perhaps, that integrating the stereotypes of their social group into their personal identity (in the form of who they don't want to be) would lead to reinforcing those very same stereotypes. These students drew stark attention to the ways in which race and racism influence the development of personal and social identities.

The identity development of the Chinese American youth was primarily a process of accommodating to the climate in which others were telling them that they were not worthy. Although sometimes there were signs of resistance, their narratives suggested that they had fully internalized the negative portrayal of Chinese Americans.

These patterns of resistance and accommodation in identity development are a reflection of the larger political and social context of the United
States in which light skin is valued over dark skin, native-born Americans
are valued over immigrants, and assertiveness is valued over shyness. It is
also the context of New York City, where Puerto Ricans have little political
or economic clout but they do have forms of celebrations (for example, the
Puerto Rican Parade) that the city is willing to support each year and which
reinforces both Puerto Rican pride and the idealization of Puerto Rican students by their non–Puerto Rican peers.

Our findings also suggest that the consequences of identity development
may vary by context. Having pride in one's ethnic group, for example, may be
substantially different across ethnic groups depending on the context. Maintaining a sense of pride about one's ethnic group for the Chinese American
adolescents, for example, will likely lead to (and may stem from) a much more
confident sense of self than among, for example, the Puerto Rican students.
Resisting a negative climate will likely be linked to mental health in ways that
accommodating to a positive climate will not (Brown & Gilligan, 1992). In
fact, we found in our survey data that feelings of attachment to one's ethnic
group is more strongly related to psychological adjustment for the African
American, Chinese American, and the Dominican students than the Puerto
Rican students (see Pahl & Way, 2006). Our quantitative and qualitative findings suggest that in order to understand the correlates of ethnic identity, it is
critical to understand the process of identity development and how the contexts, such as the social hierarchy of the school, shape these processes.

Our findings also underscore the importance of moving beyond a
numerical definition of context in studies of schools and ethnic identity.
Rather than reflecting the numbers of students from different ethnic groups
within a school, the relational dynamics or social hierarchy within the school
represent the political, social, and economic context of the school and of the
city in which the school was located. The fact that the Chinese students were
the largest ethnic group in the school but were on the bottom of the social
hierarchy suggests that the larger context of the school and city played a more
important role in determining how they were perceived than their numerical
representation in the school. We would not expect Puerto Rican or Chinese
American students who live in other cities or attend different high schools to
sound the same, and the correlates of ethnic identity would not necessarily
be the same. The meaning or implications of resistance and of accommodation reflect the context, and thus, studying the context and the relational
processes that provide meaning to the context is essential for understanding
identity development. Future studies need to move beyond simply showing
the correlation between levels of ethnic identity and adjustment and begin to
explore how variations in the form and content of identity development are
shaped by the context and provide insight into the ways in which identity
development may be linked to psychological adjustment.

NEW DIRECTIONS FOR CHILD AND ADOLESCENT DEVELOPMENT • DOI: 10.1002/cd

References

Adler, P. A., & Adler, P. (1987). Membership roles in field research. Thousand Oaks, CA: Sage.

Bronfenbrenner, U. (1979). Ecological systems theory. Annals of Child Development, 6, 187–249.

Brown, L. M., & Gilligan, C. (1992). Meeting at the crossroads: Women's psychology and girls' development. Cambridge, MA: Harvard University Press.

Cooper, C. (1999). Multiple selves, multiple worlds: Cultural perspectives on individuality and connectedness in adolescent development. In A. S. Masten (Ed.), Cultural processes in child development: The Minnesota Symposia on Child Psychology, Vol. 29 (pp. 25–57). Mahwah, NJ: Erlbaum.

Erikson, E. H. (1968). Identity: Youth and crisis. New York: Norton.

French, S., Seidman, E., Allen, L., & Aber, L. (2000). Racial/ethnic identity, congruence with the social context, and the transition to high school. Journal of Adolescent Research, 15(5), 587–602.

Helms, J. E. (1990). Black and White racial identity: theory, research, and practice. Westport, CT: Greenwood Press.

Lofland, J., & Lofland, L. H. (1995). Analyzing social settings: A guide to qualitative observation and analysis. Belmont, CA: Wadsworth.

Miller, B. (1991). Adolescents' relationships with their friends. Unpublished doctoral dissertation, Harvard University.

Niemann, Y., Romero, A., Arredondo, J., & Rodriguez, V. (1999). What does it mean to be "Mexican"? Social construction of an ethnic identity. Hispanic Journal of Behavioral Sciences, 21(1), 47–60.

Pahl, K., & Way, N. (2006). Longitudinal trajectories of ethnic identity among urban Black and Latino adolescents. Child Development, 77, 1403–1415.

Phinney, J. (1990). Ethnic identity in adolescents and adults: Review of research. Psychological Bulletin, 108, 499–514.

Phinney, J., Cantu, C., & Kurtz, D. (1997). Ethnic and American identity as predictors of self esteem among African-American, Latino, and White adolescents. Journal of Youth and Adolescence, 26(2), 165–185.

Phinney S. J., & Rotheram, J. M. (1987). Children's ethnic socialization pluralism and development. Thousand Oaks, CA: Sage.

Phinney, J. S., & Tarver, S. (1988). Ethnic identity search and commitment in Black and White eighth graders. Journal of Early Adolescence, 8(3), 265–277.

Portes, A., & Rumbaut, G. R. (2001). Legacies: The story of the immigrant second generation. New York and Berkeley: Russell Sage Foundation and University of California Press.

Qin, D., & Way, N. (in press). The family and peer contexts of Chinese American adolescents. Youth and Society.

Rosenbloom, S. R., & Way, N. (2004). Experiences of discrimination among African American, Asian American, and Latino adolescents in an urban high school. Youth and Society, 35(4), 420–451.

Rumbaut, R. (2005). Sites of belonging: Acculturation, discrimination, and ethnic identity among children of immigrants. In T. Weisner (Ed.), Discovering successful pathways in children's development: Mixed methods in the study of childhood and family life. Chicago: University of Chicago Press.

Strauss, A., & Corbin, J. (1990). Basics of qualitative research: Grounded theory procedures and techniques. Thousand Oaks, CA: Sage.

Tajfel, H. (1978). The social psychology of minorities. New York: Minority Rights Group.

Tamis-Lemonda, C. S., Way, N., Yoshikawa, H., Hughes, D., & Niwa, E. Y. (2008). A new view of individualism and collectivism across cultures and context. Social Development.

Torres, V., & Magolda, M. B. (2004). Reconstructing Latino identity: The influence of cognitive development on the ethnic identity process of Latino students. *Journal of College Student Development, 45*(3), 333–347.

Umaña-Taylor, A. (2003). Ethnic identity and self-esteem: Examining the role of social context. *Journal of Adolescence, 27,* 139–146.

Verkuyten, M. (2005). *The social psychology of ethnic identity.* New York: Routledge.

Way, N. (1998). *Everyday courage: The stories and lives of urban teenagers.* New York: New York University Press.

Way, N., Kim, C., & Santos, C. (2005). *A contextualized understanding of the experience of ethnic identity.* Paper presented at the annual meeting of the Society for Research in Child Development, Atlanta, GA.

Wilkins, A. (2004). Puerto Rican wannabes: Sexual spectacle and the marking of race, class, and gender boundaries. *Gender and Society, 18*(1), 103–121.

Yip, T., Seaton, E., & Sellers, R. (2006). African American racial identity across the life-span: Identity status, identity content, and depressive symptoms. *Child Development, 77,* 504–517.

NIOBE WAY *is professor of applied psychology and director of the developmental psychology program at New York University.*

CARLOS SANTOS *is a doctoral candidate in developmental psychology in the Department of Applied Psychology at New York University.*

ERIKA Y. NIWA *is a doctoral candidate in developmental psychology in the Department of Applied Psychology at New York University.*

CONSTANCE KIM-GERVEY *is a doctoral candidate in developmental psychology in the Department of Applied Psychology at New York University.*

Orbe, M. P. (2008). Theorizing multidimensional identity negotiation: Reflections on the lived experiences of first-generation college students. In M. Azmitia, M. Syed, & K. Radmacher (Eds.), *The intersections of personal and social identities. New Directions for Child and Adolescent Development, 120,* 81–95.

6

Theorizing Multidimensional Identity Negotiation: Reflections on the Lived Experiences of First-Generation College Students

Mark P. Orbe

Abstract

Drawing from recent research on first-generation college (FGC) students, this chapter advances an interdisciplinary theoretical framework for understanding how these students enact multiple aspects of their personal, cultural, and social identities. I use dialectical and cross-cultural adaptation theories as a foundation to extend examinations of how diverse FGC students negotiate the alien culture of the academy against that of home. In this regard, college is situated as a pivotal point of development, and successful negotiation of identity tensions is represented as a key factor in academic success. © Wiley Periodicals, Inc.

Over time, first-generation college students have received increased attention from researchers (Terenzini, Springer, Yaeger, Pascarella, & Nora, 1996). The most recent data collected by the National Center for Education Statistics (2001) and the Pell Institute for the Study of Opportunity in Higher Education (Engle, Bermeo, & O'Brien, 2006) confirm the grim reality for FGC students: compared to students who have at least one parent with a college degree, they are significantly less likely to go to college and, once on campus, less likely to persist to graduation. According to Engle et al. (2006), this reality is due to poor academic preparation, lower educational aspirations, less encouragement and support from family, less knowledge about the college application process, fewer resources to pay for college, and difficulties adjusting to the academic, social, and cultural norms of the academy.

The majority of published research on FGC students has used quantitative methodologies to produce generalizations about this heterogeneous group. The model described here extends recent research that has used qualitative inquiry to draw attention to how these generalizations vary greatly for individual FGC students.

Traditionally, scholars in the field of education have produced a growing body of literature on FGC students that has focused on academic success (Riehl, 1994; York-Anderson & Bowman, 1991; Zwerling & London, 1992). Although this literature has represented the vast majority of scholarly inquiry in this area, recent research in the field of communication has begun to explore the complexities of FGC student identity negotiation specifically by using rigorous qualitative processes to reveal thick descriptions of lived experience (Orbe, 2003, 2004, 2006; Orbe & Groscurth, 2004; Putman & Thompson, 2006). Drawing on insights from these previous studies, this chapter advances a theoretical framework for understanding how FGC students enact multiple aspects of their personal, cultural, and social identities. In particular, it examines how FGC students negotiate the alien culture of the academy against that of home.

This chapter is based on two assumptions. First, attending college represents a time of significant identity negotiation for FGC students. Second, all FGC students will experience a similar set of dialectical tensions at home and on campus; however, the particular constellation and magnitude of the tensions will vary contingent on personal, social, and cultural realities. Given these assumptions, dialectical and cross-cultural adaptation theories serve as the foundation for this work.

Theoretical Foundations

Dialectical theory is traced to Mikhail Bakhtin's theory of dialogism, which conceptualizes social life as an open dialogue. In particular, Bakhtin (1981) posited that social interaction is "a contradiction ridden, tension filled unity of two embattled tendencies" (p. 272). Bakhtin's ideas have been used in

NEW DIRECTIONS FOR CHILD AND ADOLESCENT DEVELOPMENT • DOI: 10.1002/cd

various disciplines: ethnic and feminist studies, education, philosophy, psychology, and sociology. Communication scholars (Baxter & Montgomery, 1996; Martin & Nakayama, 1999; Montgomery & Baxter, 1998) have adopted these ideas in the creation of a dialectical perspective that focuses on how individuals use communication practices to negotiate the contradictions inherent in everyday life. Contradictions revolve around particular dialectical tensions that reflect "the dynamic interplay between unified opposites" (Montgomery & Baxter, 1998, p. 4). In their most basic form, dialectical tensions reflect opposing constructs, both of which are deemed necessary, valuable, and desirable. Accordingly, dialectical theory is grounded within a both-and rather than an either-or conceptualization of social life (Baxter, Braithwaite, Bryant, & Wagner, 2004). In other words, both sides of dialectical tensions are always present, and it is the constant negotiation of these tensions that leads to relational growth, personal transformation, or both (Baxter, 2006).

While dialectical theory has gained significant prominence in research in and out of the field of communication, it has seldom been used as a foundation for exploring identity negotiation specifically (but see Tappan & Brown, Chapter Four, and Penuel & Wertsch, 1995). Throughout this chapter, I argue that a dialectical approach to FGC student identity negotiation reflects an innovative approach that recognizes the multidimensionality of a complex process. As a means to unite dialectical theory and identity in more concrete ways, I turn to a theory that provides insight into identity negotiation that occurs as individuals move from one culture to another.

Cross-cultural adaptation theory was initially created to capture the experiences of travelers, immigrants, and sojourners as they ventured into unfamiliar cultural terrain (Kim, 1988). In this context, adaptation refers to "the entirety of the evolutionary process an individual undergoes vis-à-vis a new and unfamiliar environment" (Kim, 2005, p. 379). Situating adaptation within the intersection of the person and environment, cross-cultural adaptation theory focuses on the communicative process through which individuals interactively negotiate their changing identities. According to the theory, "even relatively short-term sojourners must be at least minimally concerned with building a healthy functional relationship with the host environment in ways similar to the native population" (Kim, 2005, p. 375). Conceptually this process is one that has direct application for FGC students.

One of the key concepts central to cross-cultural adaptation theory is the stress-adaptation-growth dynamic. According to this idea, an unfamiliar environment triggers stress in the individual psyche fueled by a need to change and yet remain the same. Consistent with the premise of balance theories (Festinger, 1957), change and stress are inextricably linked: "Each experience of adaptive change inevitably accompanies stress in the individual psyche—a kind of identity conflict rooted in resistance to change: the desire to retain old customs in keeping with the original identity, on the one hand, and the desire to change behavior in seeking harmony with the new milieu, on the other" (Kim, 2005, p. 383).

Adaptation in this context is seen as the effective management of this stress. Cross-cultural adaptation theory posits that the outcome of the stress-adaptation disequilibrium is growth over time. This process reflects dialectic, cyclic, and continual movement between experiences of stress and adaptation, which ultimately leads to an emergent identity inclusive of both new and old selves.

FGC Identity Negotiation: Six Primary Dialectical Tensions

The fundamental idea of this chapter is that identity takes shape amid "the interplay of conflicting and interconnected forces" (Montgomery, 1993, p. 206). These forces, or dialectical tensions, are inherently neither good nor bad and exist on a continuum where there is no balancing point, no center, no equilibrium—only flux (Baxter, 2004). This chapter explicates six primary and twelve secondary dialectical tensions that are at the core of FGC student identity negotiation (see Table 6.1). Through descriptions of these tensions, I illustrate how FGC student status, from the perspective of FGC students themselves, interacts with other aspects of identity. These tensions are presented in a linear manner; however, given the inseparability of contradictions (Montgomery & Baxter, 1998), some interconnectivity among tensions is inevitable.

Individual ↔ Social Identity. Developing a sense of self requires that individuals negotiate their personal identities within larger social groups to which they belong (Tajfel, 1981; Turner, 1991). Consequently, identities simultaneously revolve around both individual and social aspects of identification. This primary dialectical tension, then, reflects the struggle between an individual (personal) and social (collective) self-concept (see also Brewer, 1991; Chapter Two, this volume). The opposing forces within this contradiction are central to the experiences of FGC students; however, they are manifested differently while at home versus while on campus.

Independence ↔ Interdependence. When at home, the individual ↔ social identity tension is best understood as a struggle between independence and interdependence. Both opposing poles are important and necessary for healthy self-concepts and adaptation to college. FGC students have a need to create distance between themselves and their family members, yet they also must maintain some level of closeness.

The need to establish an identity separate from one's family is a natural outgrowth of the transition from adolescence to adulthood (see Erikson, 1968). For FGC students, going to college, especially when they live in on- or off-campus housing, represents an opportunity to construct an independent identity, that is, to individuate. The dialectical tension at home exists when students return home with a more individualistic sense of self and are confronted with family members who do not accept their new sense of independence. FGC students are individuals, but they also see themselves as

Table 6.1. First-Generation College Student Dialectical Tensions

Primary Dialectical Tensions	Secondary Tensions Negotiated at Home	Secondary Tensions Negotiated on Campus
Individual ↔ Social Identity	Independence ↔ Interdependence	Autonomy ↔ Connection
Similar ↔ Different	Ordinary ↔ Special	Peripheral ↔ Central
Stability ↔ Change	Old ↔ New	Divergence ↔ Convergence
Certainty ↔ Uncertainty	Predictability ↔ Unpredictability	Confidence ↔ Doubt
Advantage ↔ Disadvantage	Support ↔ Resistance	Motivation ↔ Pressure
Openness ↔ Closedness	Reveal ↔ Conceal	Visible ↔ Invisible

NEW DIRECTIONS FOR CHILD AND ADOLESCENT DEVELOPMENT • DOI: 10.1002/cd

inextricably linked to family and community. Part of the interdependent nature of identity can be seen in terms of the collective pride that surrounds FGC students; this is most evident by the vast amount of college paraphernalia that family members own and the tendency to tout their child's success to anyone who will listen (Orbe, 2003). FGC students understand, and appreciate, how their success is interconnected with that of their extended family; this, however, is contrasted with needs of independence. Gender, race/ethnicity, and nationality seem to affect how FGC students negotiate this tension; for example, those from more collectivistic cultures feel a greater pull to the social aspect of their identities.

Autonomy ↔ *Connection.* On campus, the primary tension of personal ↔ social identity is best conceptualized as a negotiation of autonomy and connection (see also Grotevant & Cooper, 1998). For many, including FGC students, attending college represents a significant opportunity to avert family influences and be seen as an individual. Consistent with the values of Western society, FGC students value a sense of autonomy. Although maintaining a certain sense of autonomy in college is desirable, it is juxtaposed against a need to connect with others.

Like others, FGC students quickly learn that collegiate success is contingent on their ability to connect with others: working collaboratively with other students, developing mentoring relationships with faculty and administrators, networking with alumni and other professionals in their chosen field, and seeking support from the larger community (Orbe, 2004). Depending on the most salient aspects of their identities, FGC students seek to connect with others who share similar life experiences or goals (examples are university support programs, cultural groups, places of worship, and professional organizations). Within these associations, they are able to interact with people who are both similar and different to them.

Similar ↔ **Different.** Inherent within a dialectical approach to identity is a recognition that all humans are simultaneously similar and different (Martin & Nakayama, 1999). Therefore, while this chapter focuses on the common experiences of FGC students, it also acknowledges the diversity within this large, heterogeneous group by drawing significant attention to how these students vary in terms of race, gender, socioeconomic status, and age. As such, the theoretical framework presented here attempts to resist the tendency to overemphasize intergroup differences and intragroup similarities. This scholarly tension is also one that affects FGC students in terms of how they communicate and perform their identities at home and on campus.

Ordinary ↔ *Special.* For FGC students, home represents a retreat from school—a space where they can feel comfortable around others like them. Relationships at home are defined primarily in terms of similarity and familiarity; as such, FGC students often seek refuge at home (and within their home communities) as an escape from the stress of collegiate life. Being ordinary at home often competes with the reality that FGC students also must negotiate the special status that is afforded to them. They are often given significant attention by family members and others in their communities. This includes being asked to speak to younger students about college, having special meals cooked especially for them, being recognized during church services, and even benefiting from monetary gifts from others (Orbe, 2003). In many ways, FGC students are treated differently from their siblings, a treatment that leads to the negotiation of additional tensions at home.

Peripheral ↔ Central. At the core of theorizing identity negotiation is the recognition that FGC student status is only one of many aspects of an individual's sense of self. Accordingly, an inherent tension revolves around the saliency of being the first in one's family to attend college. FGC student status is situated as a peripheral aspect of one's identity. In this regard, other cultural identity markers can be seen as most salient to a person's identity; these include race/ethnicity, socioeconomic status, gender, age, sexual orientation, and nationality. Situating FGC identity on the periphery seems most apparent for those individuals who (1) attend colleges where the majority of students were the first in their families to go to college or (2) benefit from the privileges of majority group status in other ways—race, class, or gender, for example (Orbe, 2004).

FGC student identity, like that of all other humans, is multidimensional. For some, the fact that they are the first in their families to attend college is viewed as less central to their self-concept when compared to other identity markers like race, socioeconomic status, and age. In contrast, FGC student status occupies a central place in one's sense of self, especially as it occurs on college campuses when the majority is presumed to come from more educated families. Accordingly, the educational experiences of FGC students are filled with instances where they are reminded of their unique standing in college, something that leads to greater identity saliency. The reality is that the saliency of being an FGC student on campus is constantly in flux. Identifying (or being defined) as a first-generation college student triggers a certain sense of pride, humility, and purpose (Putman & Thompson, 2006). However, identifying only as such is limiting in that it renders other aspects of one's identity as inconsequential.

Stability ↔ Change. This primary dialectical tension highlights the dualistic way in which a person's identity is consistent over time yet constantly changing as we grow older (Erikson, 1968; Hogg & Abrams, 1988). For FGC students, this tension is seen in the ways that they seek constancy and familiarity in their lives, while desiring the stimulation that comes with novelty and change. As the first person in their families to attend college, they experience the stability ↔ change tension at home and on campus.

Old ↔ New. FGC students, especially when returning home after spending time away in college, experience a struggle between their "old" and "new" selves (see also Azmitia, Syed, & Radmacher, Chapter One). At the core of the collegiate experience is an enhanced knowledge of self; in the process, one's identity undergoes significant change. Because of this, an inherent tension for

FGC students at home is negotiating the changes that come with a college education in a context where others do not share that experience. In this regard, there is a constant negotiation of established and emerging identities.

While FGC students may be largely unconscious of their emerging new identities, others at home are not. FGC students report that family members accuse them of "thinking that they are better than others" or "forgetting who they are" (quoted in Orbe, 2006). This appears to be an issue for all but seems most pronounced for FGC students of color, who were often accused of "acting white" or "selling out" (Orbe, 2003). Not allowing college to change one's established identity is important to FGC students (as well as their families), but it is also unrealistic given the nature of higher education. Nevertheless, one thing remains clear: unsuccessful negotiation of old and new identities has grave consequences, including the isolation of family members and close friends and the students themselves.

Divergence ↔ Convergence. On campus, the stability ↔ change tension takes the form of FGC student divergence ↔ convergence. This secondary tension relates specifically to the communication styles of FGC students: divergence refers to communicative behaviors that emphasize outgroup status, whereas convergence involves communication that mirrors that of the majority group (see Gallois, Ogay, & Giles, 2005). Inherent within this tension is the necessity for FGC students to negotiate communication systems that reflect both their old and new identities in ways that are appropriate, authentic, and effective. In other words, they must work to enact a communicative voice that, depending on the situation, converges or diverges with the college culture.

While both polar opposites in this secondary tension are integral for collegiate success or just survival, convergence appears to be more accessible for European American students whose FGC status (and in some cases, socioeconomic status) is less salient than other identity characteristics (Orbe, 2004). When FGC student status intersects with other aspects of an individual's identity that position a person as an outsider (for example, based on age, race, or ethnicity), divergence is dominant. For instance, when African American and Latino FGC students are a distinct minority on campus, they may experience a sense of hypervisibility where they are often defined through preconceived racial and ethnic stereotypes (Chapter One, this volume; Orbe, 2003, 2006). Because of this, some seek to assimilate into the culture of the academy by mirroring the dress, language, and behaviors of the majority. At other times, they might embrace their FGC student status and consciously avoid assimilation, working to maintain the uniqueness of their experience and highlighting how their perspective contributes to a diverse learning experience. In doing so, they focus on "representing," that is, being sure that others see the positive aspects of their life experiences.

Certainty ↔ Uncertainty. Humans by nature have a need for constancy in their lives and find comfort in being able to count on certain routines and roles (Festinger, 1957). However, life with too much certainty leads to feelings of boredom, monotony, or stagnation. Accordingly, they also seek the excitement that comes with new experiences. In a nutshell, this dialectical tension (like others) includes polar opposites that are necessary, satisfying, and desirable. For FGC students, the novelty of the collegiate experience brings to the foreground a number of specific struggles.

Predictability ↔ *Unpredictability.* Home represents a location that is safe and comfortable, in large part due to its predictability. In retrospect, what FGC students fail to recognize is that they were not always able to predict how going to college would change life at home. Although it appears illogical and contradictory, students want their home life to be predictable in its routine as well as unpredictable in terms of the uncertainty that comes changing family dynamics.

While home may continue to remain a place with clear routines, FGC students quickly realize that their status as educational trailblazers prompts some unpredictability when it comes to established roles (Putman & Thompson, 2006). For instance, FGC students are often asked to assume the role of mentor, advisor, or expert in their families (and, in some instances, larger communities). For some, this responsibility is simply an extension of established roles; for others, it is a new aspect of their familial positionality that may come at the expense of older family members. Generally FGC students desire to embrace and thrive in their new roles. The struggle is in how they simultaneously seek the predictability that comes with home alongside the unpredictability that is inherent in new family dynamics.

Confidence ↔ *Doubt.* As articulated by one FGC student, "confidence is a learned behavior" (quoted in Orbe, 2003). For many, confidence is established through an accomplished high school record, overcoming significant life obstacles, or meaningful interactions with mentors. Despite a significant amount of confidence, the transition to college inevitably triggers feelings of doubt. FGC students question if they will fit in with other students, handle college-level work, and balance the stressors associated with school, family, and work.

Some might believe that being successful at the beginning of college would eliminate the doubt that exists for FGC students. True to the philosophical assumptions of dialogism, however, the dialectical tension of confidence ↔ doubt requires ongoing negotiation. For example, while early collegiate success increases the confidence of FGC students, it does little to diminish the doubt that exists when they take on new challenges, such as upper-level classes or graduate school. In fact, FGC students describe suffering from an ever-present "imposter complex." At each stage of their academic experience, they feel as if they are unqualified and simply posing as a member of the academic community; at any time, they will be "found out" and exposed for who they really are. While some may regard doubt as undesirable, FGC students understand it as an important source of constant motivation (Orbe, 2004).

Advantage ↔ Disadvantage. Privilege and penalty are inherent to the experiences of FGC students (Collins, 1990). In many ways, they are privileged to have opportunities that other family members have not had; because of this, they do not take the educational opportunities afforded to them for granted. Despite this, FGC students also experience disadvantage at home and on campus. Part of the disadvantage at home relates to being situated as different from others; on campus, unlike non-FGC students, they do not benefit from getting specific advice from parents or having family understand the pressures of college (see Chapter One). These issues, inherent in the advantage ↔ disadvantage tension, are examined further in terms of the particular contexts of home and campus.

Support ↔ Resistance. Almost without exception, FGC students identify their families as key sources of support for their college success (Orbe, 2004). Most point directly to their parents, yet a significant number also recognize older siblings, grandparents, aunts and uncles, and adopted parents as foundations for support. This support can take the form of emotional (pride and encouragement), physical (money, toaster ovens, fridges, blankets, and other necessities), and logistical support (like taking them to and from campus). For some nontraditional students, both women and men, general support takes the form of help with household duties. Yet, not all FGC students receive the same amount of consistent support from home; in some instances, family members seem to simultaneously support and resist their collegiate success.

While families are often verbally supportive of FGC students' attempt to use education to better their lives, their behaviors seem to tell a different story. For some, explicit support is tainted with an implicit desire for the student to fail. The source of this support ↔ resistance tension is in the reality that family members may be both proud and envious of the student's opportunities. On the part of family members, part of this resistance appears to be related to the FGC student's college experience being perceived as affecting the family negatively. This can be seen within traditional Mexican American family culture where young adults are expected to contribute financially to the family household (Putman & Thompson, 2006). Attending college, within this cultural context, may be simultaneously supported (especially in terms of the potential of ultimate financial gain) and resisted (in the light of existing finances).

Motivation ↔ Pressure. Being an FGC student on a college campus involves negotiating an inherent tension between motivation and pressure. The motivation comes from an understanding that parents and other relatives were not able to attend college. In fact, feeling as if they are representing their families (and in the case of FGC students of color, larger communities) serves as a huge source of motivation (Orbe, 2003, 2006). Descriptions from FGC students reveal that most, if not all, understand the sacrifices that parents, grandparents, and others made for them to have opportunities unavailable to those of earlier generations. Because of this, FGC students are motivated

NEW DIRECTIONS FOR CHILD AND ADOLESCENT DEVELOPMENT • DOI: 10.1002/cd

to succeed in ways that will honor ancestors and lead to the educational success of future generations.

While the unique positioning of FGC students within their families and communities works to inspire them to success, it also comes with some significant pressure. The reality of this pressure seems to be constant, yet it was especially clear when individual behaviors do not match the expectations of others. Expectations, in this context, do not simply revolve around academic progress, good grades, or graduation. They can also involve heightened social expectations that create an impression that FGC students must always present themselves in the most positive light possible. Consequently, the pressure for maximized success, especially given that these individuals are the only ones in their families to make it to college, can be intense.

Openness ↔ Closedness. This final primary dialectical tension reflects a natural desire to be open and share with others, on the one hand, and to be closed and private, on the other (Altman, 1975). FGC students, like others, want to share their experiences as a means to connect and develop relationships. Simultaneously, however, is a need to keep some things private, especially those things that might make them vulnerable to personal criticism or harm (see also Goffman, 1963).

Reveal ↔ Conceal. While at home, FGC students must simultaneously negotiate a desire to reveal certain aspects of their collegiate experience and a need to keep some matters to themselves. While family members often ask about how students are managing their lives while away from home, an inherent tension exists between what should be shared and what should not. For instance, parents often ask, "How are things going?" Some students understand that parents are interested in hearing details about all aspects of their college experience, while others are interested only in academics. Other students are quick to learn that any response other than "fine" is less than appropriate.

For some FGC students, college is not a topic that is discussed in their home. Instead, they receive clear messages that while they are at home, family matters should be the top priority. This seems to be especially true for female FGC students whose gendered roles bear on what they should reveal or conceal. For instance, Orbe (2006) described how some women raised in traditional Mexican families develop a more political "Chicana" identity that they must discard whenever they return home. Nontraditionally aged women also experience struggles with the reveal ↔ conceal dialectical tension. For example, some women who live with significant others who do not support their college aspirations reportedly do not reveal anything about their studies to them. In fact, some can study only when their partners are not home (Orbe, 2004).

Visible ↔ Invisible. Being open about one's familial educational experiences, and in the process maintaining a visibility of FGC student issues on campus, is important. For students who identify strongly with being an FGC student, sharing their experiences with others represents an important aspect of self-expression. The struggle is negotiating a need to make one's field of experience visible with an opposing desire to just assimilate.

Ideally, being the first person in one's family to attend college should be viewed as an extremely positive aspect of one's identity. Creating visibility for the experiences of being a FGC student is desirous because it helps contribute diverse perspectives to the learning community; it also works to challenge structures that falsely make assumptions about students' lived experiences. As such, one might surmise that FGC students would be open about this significant part of their identity. However, given the statistical data provided at the beginning of this chapter, FGC student status has a negative stigma on many campuses. Making this aspect of his or her identity known to others may result in (mis)perceptions that the student is ill prepared for college-level academics, without substantial educational aspirations, socially or communicatively inept, and less committed to participating fully in the learning process. Accordingly, FGC students do not feel a need to highlight that aspect of their identity. As one stated, "I don't want pity or praise for that, I want it for me. First-generation college student . . . that's not how I want to be known. I just want to be known as me, myself" (quoted in Orbe, 2004, p. 143).

Conclusion

Drawing from key concepts across a number of scholarly disciplines, this chapter builds a theoretical model stemming from the tenets of dialectical and cross-cultural adaptation theories. As such, it advances a framework that seeks to provide an understanding into the complex ways in which FGC students negotiate and perform multiple aspects of their identities. In particular, six primary dialectical tensions—individual ↔ social identity, similar ↔ different, stability ↔change, certainty ↔ uncertainty, advantage ↔ disadvantage, openness ↔ closedness—are briefly explained through how they are negotiated at home and on campus. While each of these tensions is important for understanding the experiences of FGC students, two appear explicitly relevant to identity negotiation: (1) individual ↔ social identity and (2) stability ↔ change. In this regard, the theoretical model provides a framework to understand how the personal and social identities of FGC students are negotiated over time amid a number of other tensions. While this chapter focused on one aspect of identity (FGC student status), a third primary tension, similar ↔ different, draws attention to the intersectionality that is inherent in identity negotiation. In fact, one secondary tension, that of peripheral ↔ central, speaks to the necessity of understanding identity negotiation as a complex process experienced by multidimensional beings who cannot be effectively understood through analyses that acknowledge only one aspect of identity.

Understanding identity as an ongoing negotiation of dialectical tensions that ultimately can lead to positive growth represents an innovative, productive lens for scholars across disciplines. While FGC student status is the focus of this chapter, particular attention has been paid to how this aspect of identity is negotiated alongside other identity markers based on race, gender, socioeconomic status, and age. While the significance of being the first in their families to attend college may make the tensions more explicit for FGC students, all students negotiate these tensions in similar yet different ways, often related to other cultural identity markers. Accordingly, additional research and theorizing can create frameworks that are more general (for example, college students) or more specific (African American inner-city male students) and explore how identity negotiation is affected by contextual elements inherent in various environments, including those associated with home and campus.

Implicit throughout this chapter is the assumption that college represents a pivotal time in the development of emerging adult identity (see also Chapter One). The theoretical model introduced here suggests that for FGC students, successful negotiation of the tensions that come with new aspects of their identities is crucial to collegiate success in terms of both academic and social arenas. Consistent with other scholarship on dialogism (Baxter, 2004), the first stage of this work has identified the specific tensions associated with dualism. The next stage is to explore dialectical strategies, that is, effective communication practices, used to manage these tensions in productive, satisfying ways. Given space limitations, I was not able to focus the role that particular communication practices play in cultivating a successful college experience for FGC students. However, scholars can draw from some preliminary work in this area (Orbe & Groscurth, 2004) as they continue to explore the complex nature of identity negotiation from an interdisciplinary perspective. In fact, this may be a primary area through which communication scholars can contribute to ongoing discussions with colleagues from psychology, sociology, education, and other related fields.

References

Altman, I. (1975). *The environment and social behavior: Privacy, personal space, territory, and crowding*. Belmont, CA: Wadsworth.

Bakhtin, M. M. (1981). *The dialogic imagination: Four essays*. Austin: University of Texas Press.

Baxter, L. A. (2004). A tale of two voices: Relational dialectics theory. *Journal of Family Communication, 4*, 181–192.

Baxter, L. A. (2006). Relational dialectics theory: Multivocal dialogues of family communication. In D. O. Braithwaite & L. A. Baxter (Eds.), *Engaging theories in family communication: Multiple perspectives* (pp. 130–145). Thousand Oaks, CA: Sage.

Baxter, L. A., Braithwaite, D. O., Bryant, L., & Wagner, A. (2004). Stepchildren's perceptions of the contradictions in communication with stepparents. *Journal of Social and Personal Relationships, 21*(4), 447–467.

Baxter, L. A., & Montgomery, B. M. (Eds.). (1996). *Relating: Dialogues and dialectics*. New York: Guilford Press.

Brewer, M. B. (1991). The social self: On being the same and different at the same time. *Personality and Social Psychology Bulletin, 17*, 475–482.

Collins, P. H. (1990). *Black feminist thought: Knowledge, consciousness, and the politics of empowerment*. Boston: Unwin Hyman.

94 THE INTERSECTIONS OF PERSONAL AND SOCIAL IDENTITIES

Engle, J., Bermeo, A., & O'Brien, C. (2006). *Straight from the source: What works for first-generation college students.* Washington, DC: Pell Institute for the Study of Opportunity in Higher Education.

Erikson, E. (1968). *Identity: Youth and crisis.* New York: Basic Books.

Festinger, L. (1957). *A theory of cognitive dissonance.* Stanford, CA: Stanford University Press.

Gallois, C., Ogay, T., & Giles, H. (2005). Communication accommodation theory. In W. B. Gudykunst (Ed.), *Theorizing about intercultural communication* (pp. 121–148). Thousand Oaks, CA: Sage.

Goffman, E. (1963). *Stigma: Notes on the management of spoiled identities.* Upper Saddle River, NJ: Prentice Hall.

Grotevant, H. D., & Cooper, C. R. (1998). Individuality and connectedness in adolescent development. Review and prospects for research on identity, relationships, and context. In E.E.A. Skoe & A. L. von der Lippe (Eds.), *Personality development in adolescence: Cross national and life span perspectives* (pp. 3–37). Florence, KY: Taylor & Francis/Routledge.

Hogg, M. A., & Abrams, D. (1988). *Social identifications: A social psychology of intergroup relations and group processes.* London: Routledge.

Kim, Y. Y. (1988). *Communication and cross-cultural adaptation: An integrative theory.* Clevendon, UK: Multilingual Matters.

Kim, Y. Y. (2005). Adapting to a new culture: An integrative communication theory. In W. B. Gudykunst (Ed.), *Theorizing about intercultural communication* (pp. 375–400). Thousand Oaks, CA: Sage.

Martin, J. N., & Nakayama, T. (1999). Thinking dialectically about culture and communication. *Communication Theory, 9*(1), 1–25.

Montgomery, B. M. (1993). Relationship maintenance versus relationship change: A dialectical dilemma. *Journal of Social and Personal Relationships, 10,* 205–223.

Montgomery, B. M., & Baxter, L. A. (1998). A guide to dialectical approaches to studying personal relationships. In B. Montgomery & L. A. Baxter (Eds.), *Dialectical approaches to studying personal relationships* (pp. 1–16). Mahwah, NJ: Erlbaum.

National Center for Education Statistics. (2001). *First-generation students: Undergraduates whose parents never enrolled in postsecondary education.* Retrieved December 15, 2006, from http://nces.ed.gov/pubs98/98082.htm.

Orbe, M. (2003). African American first generation college student communicative experiences. *Electronic Journal of Communication/La Revue Electronique de Communication, 13*(2/3). http:www.cios.org/www/ejc/v013n2toc.htm.

Orbe, M. (2004). Negotiating multiple identities within multiple frames: An analysis of first generation college students. *Communication Education, 53*(2), 131–149.

Orbe, M. (2006, December). *Latino/a first-generation college students: Similarities and differences across predominantly Latino and predominantly white campuses.* Paper presented at the annual meeting of the Speech Communication Association of Puerto Rico, San Juan, P.R.

Orbe, M., & Groscurth, C. R. (2004). A co-cultural theoretical analysis of communicating on campus and at home: Exploring the negotiation strategies of first generation college (FGC) students. *Qualitative Research Reports in Communication, 5,* 41–47.

Penuel, W. R., & Wertsch, J. V. (1995). Vygotsky and identity formation: A sociocultural approach. *Educational Psychologist, 30,* 83–92.

Putman, A., & Thompson, S. (2006). Paving the way: First-generation Mexican American community college students in a border community speak out. In M. Orbe, B. Allen, & L. Flores (Eds.), *The same and different: Acknowledging the diversity with and between cultural groups* (pp. 121–142). Washington, DC: NCA Press.

Riehl, R. J. (1994). The academic preparation, aspirations, and first-year performance of first-generation students. *College and University, 70*(1), 14–19.

Tajfel, H. (1981). *Human groups and social categories: Studies in social psychology.* Cambridge: Cambridge University Press

Terenzini, P. T., Springer, L., Yaeger, P. M., Pascarella, E. T., & Nora, A. (1996). First generation college students: Characteristics, experiences, and cognitive development. *Research in Higher Education, 37*(1), 1–22.

Turner, J. C. (1991). *Social influence.* Milton Keynes, UK: Open University Press.

York-Anderson, D. C., & Bowman, S. L. (1991). Assessing the college knowledge of first-generation and second-generation college students. *Journal of College Student Development, 32,* 116–122.

Zwerling, L. S., & London, H. B. (Eds.). (1992). *First-generation students: Confronting the cultural issues.* San Francisco: Jossey-Bass.

MARK P. ORBE is a professor of communication and diversity, with a joint appointment in the Gender and Women's Studies Program, Western Michigan University.

Phinney, J. S. (2008). Bridging identities and disciplines: Advances and challenges in understanding multiple identities. In M. Azmitia, M. Syed, & K. Radmacher (Eds.), *The intersections of personal and social identities*. New Directions for Child and Adolescent
Development, 120, 97–109.

Bridging Identities and Disciplines: Advances and Challenges in Understanding Multiple Identities

Jean S. Phinney

Abstract

*The chapters in this volume address the need for a better understanding of the
development of intersecting identities over age and context. The chapters provide valuable insights into the development of identities, particularly group identities. They highlight common processes across identities, such as the role of
contrast and comparison and the need for individual effort in identity formation. They suggest the value of studying multiple identities in interaction and
using interdisciplinary approaches. However, research across identities and disciplines poses challenges for investigators. These challenges can be met and the
field advanced by collaborative studies among scholars who represent different
disciplines and have studied different identities.* © Wiley Periodicals, Inc.

Scholars from a wide range of backgrounds have long been concerned with the concept of identity, but they have consistently had difficulty in agreeing on exactly what it is and how it can best be studied. The term is used to refer to both personal identity, concerned with a sense of self as a unique individual with particular abilities, interests, and goals, and group identity, concerned with one's membership in identified social groups or categories. (The term *group identity* is used here, instead of *social identity*, to refer to membership in an identified group, such as one's gender or ethnic group. The term *social identity* has been used in a variety of ways in psychology, to refer to both group membership and to social relationships; it therefore seems less precise to convey my meaning.) For the individual, these two types of identities are interrelated in complex ways, as the chapters in this volume suggest. The volume deals with both of these types of identity; however, group identities clearly dominate, and they are the primary focus of this chapter.

Group identities have sometimes been seen simply as the social categories to which individuals are assigned or assign themselves; for example, an African American is said to "have" a Black identity by virtue of considering him or herself or being considered by others to be Black or African American. However, there is increasing agreement that a group identity is more than the group one belongs to or the label one uses. Rather, current thinkers agree that identity is a complex, dynamic construct that develops over time as individuals strive to make sense of who they are in terms of the groups they belong to within their immediate and larger social contexts. The process of identity development takes place over extended periods of time, from childhood through adulthood, and is significantly influenced by the contexts in which individuals live. Of particular importance in this volume are three large social groupings that have a significant impact on the lives of individuals: ethnicity, gender, and class. These identities interact with each other and with personal identity and the environmental context in complex ways that are the subject of increasing interest but are still not well understood.

Accompanying recognition of the complexity of group identities is a growing interest in studying them in ways that acknowledge and attempt to deal with the multifaceted and changing nature of multiple identities over time and context. The chapters here represent a valuable step in this endeavor. They provide new insights into the development and expression of many types of identities and illustrate the range of approaches being used to study them. However, these chapters also illustrate the difficulties of trying to understand the development of intersecting identities by bridging identities and disciplines.

The volume editors focus on three dominant themes, which provide a useful framework for examining what the chapters add to our understanding of the development of multiple identities. I first discuss processes and contexts of identity development, a topic that is central to all the chapters and to which this volume makes a strong contribution. The two other key themes, interdisciplinary approaches in the study of identity development and the intersection of multiple identities, are less well understood and are reflected to varying degrees in the six chapters. In the following sections, each of these themes is discussed with reference to the ideas expressed in the chapters and related issues in the field.

Development of Group Identity in Context

Perhaps the central theme of this volume is expressed in the question: When and how do social (or group) identities develop? Developmental psychologists acknowledge that all development is a process involving the interaction of a developing individual within a context that supports or, in some cases, inhibits the process. The developmental side of the equation focuses on the cognitive and physical changes that alter the way children and adolescents think about and respond to their social environments, together with individual differences in personal characteristics and genetic makeup; the context includes the proximal and distal factors that interact with these changes, providing experiences, opportunities, role models, and limitations that shape identity formation and are themselves changed by choices the individual makes.

Normative developmental trajectories have been described for particular identities at particular points in time, but there has been little generalization over different identities and time periods. For example, a normative trajectory of understanding gender roles and stereotypes in young children has been described as consisting of stages, beginning with the construction of gender stereotypes, followed by consolidation, which peaks at ages five or six and is accompanied by rigidity in stereotypes. The next stage, integration, is accompanied by greater flexibility in the understanding of stereotypes (see Chapter Three). This normative trajectory seems driven largely by developmental factors, but variation in the timing of these stages suggests that individual differences and environmental influences play a role in the process.

Hurtado and Silva (Chapter Two) propose one possible environmental influence: that children's media provide information and models that can promote more flexible and complex thinking about group stereotypes. Hurtado and Silva emphasize the need for "reeducation" of minority children exposed to the negative stereotypes of their group in society at large as well as "reeducation" of majority children and their parents who may consciously or unconsciously adopt these negative stereotypes. The assumption is that deliberate efforts to provide positive images of social groups can play a role in the developing attitudes that children have about their social groups and those of their peers. Hurtado and Silva do not present data to show whether the TV program they describe in fact has an impact on children's identities, but it seems likely that frequent exposure to information that counteracts a stereotype could make a difference in developing attitudes.

The early attitudes and beliefs that children have about their gender, ethnicity, and other social categories become more complex as young people move into middle childhood (Ruble et al., 2004), and these attitudes serve as the underpinnings for the further development of identity in adolescence. During adolescence, young people increase in their ability to think abstractly about social groups (Quintana, 1998). At the same time, they are faced with the developmental task of constructing a personal identity (Erikson, 1968). Erikson proposes that young people must experience a period of questioning, exploring, and reflection to consolidate the sense of self developed in childhood. By reexamining and integrating their early identifications in the light of their experiences, abilities, and interests, adolescents achieve a secure sense of self, "a subjective sense of sameness and continuity" (p. 19), that provides a guide for the future. However, this process is not only internal; it takes place "in the core of the individual and yet also in the core of his communal culture" (p. 22). For Erikson, personal and group identities and the context are inextricably intertwined.

Together with the formation of a personal identity, adolescents construct group identities relative to the categories that are important and salient to them, such as gender, ethnicity, and class. The environment plays an increasingly important role in this process. Exposure to a wider world during adolescence leads to an increased awareness of group stereotypes, as well as of differences among groups in terms of power and privilege and the implications of such differences. These experiences lead to questions and uncertainty that are at the basis of identity exploration. Brown and Tappan (Chapter Four) provide a vivid example of early adolescent girls wrestling with complex issues of gender identity within the options available to them. The contradictory and emotion-laden images to which they are exposed are complex, going well beyond the stereotyped images of childhood. In a setting where the media as well as their peers support a view of fighting among girls that challenges existing notions of femininity, adolescent girls, write Brown and Tappan, "struggle with, resist, and try on differing viewpoints and values in attempts to create a sense of self." The examples they cite provide a vivid picture of these girls' efforts to negotiate the tension between a sense of self as a female and feminine stereotypes such as girls as sissies. These efforts in some cases result in their taking on stereotypically masculine behaviors and thus altering the meaning of feminine.

Along with, and often intertwined with, gender identity is the issue of ethnic identity, particularly for adolescents in ethnically diverse settings. Just as gender stereotypes provide a context for the formation of gender identities (Brown & Tappan, Chapter Four), prevailing images and attitudes within a school context are key factors in developing ethnic identities, as Way, Santos, Niwa, and Kim-Gervey show in Chapter Five. Their interviews with adolescents from four ethnic groups reveal the important role of the social climate and also highlight the very different valences of the identities of the youth from the four groups, ranging from positive to negative. This study illustrates dramatically the way in which the proximal, rather than distal, context influences ethnic identity formation, with Puerto Ricans high in the social hierarchy and Chinese low. This situation is quite different from that of many other settings, including the wider society in general, where Asians are seen more positively than Latinos. The stereotypes in the larger society appear to have little impact on these adolescents.

Way et al. report virtually no changes in the ethnic attitudes expressed in the interviews over the four years of the study, even though adolescence is considered the focal age period for identity formation. These results can be considered in relation to other research by the first author and a colleague (Pahl & Way, 2006) showing decelerating levels of ethnic identity exploration after tenth grade. It seems that these adolescents generally have accepted their position in the school hierarchy and are not actively exploring their ethnicity. For those lower in the hierarchy, this may mean not being happy with their ethnicity. Similar expressions of dissatisfaction with one's ethnicity have been reported by adolescents in other studies (Phinney, 1989). In keeping with ethnic identity development theory, these adolescents might be thought of as foreclosed (Yip, Seaton, & Sellers, 2006) or miseducated (Cross & Fhagen-Smith, 2001), in that they have accepted the negative attitudes of others about their own group without an active exploration of their own background. One wonders if exposure to appropriate programs such as *Little Bill* (described in Chapter Two) would have had an impact on these attitudes by providing alternative ways of thinking about the prevailing hierarchy. For example, social identity theory (Tajfel & Turner, 1986) suggests that individuals can counteract negative images of their groups through creative ways of redefining the bases for comparisons among groups. There is little evidence among the adolescents interviewed by Way, Santos, Niwa, and Kim-Gervey that they have questioned the existing hierarchy; however, the authors note that survey data from the study show that those who have more positive feelings of attachment to their group, presumably from rejecting the negative images they are exposed to, show better psychological adjustment.

Evidence that ethnic identity exploration continues in college (Chapter One; Phinney, 2006) suggests that the current negative ethnic identities of some of the adolescents Way et al. studied are not permanent. These adolescents have more identity work to do to gain awareness that they have choices regarding their ethnic identity. As social identity theory suggests, they can find alternative bases on which to evaluate their own and other groups and affirm the value of their own group. In particular, the Chinese and Puerto Rican youth Way and her colleagues studied may find that in later years, as they move into college or the workforce, their fortunes are reversed in terms of the valence of the prevailing stereotypes in their high school.

The issue of the stability of group identities is also raised by Brown and Tappan in Chapter Four. They emphasize that girls use cultural tools (that is, available ideologies) to enact and express their feminine identity. Because identity in this view is enacted at a particular moment in a specific context, it is seen as being fragile and unstable; it needs to be continually acted on and performed in new contexts. They interpret the results of their study as show-ing that identity is a form of mediated action that varies with the context. However, an alternative interpretation is that these girls are in what Erikson calls a moratorium period, when young people explore and try on various options as a step toward resolving the issue. Instability is characteristic of the moratorium period, but exploration is expected to lead to be a better under-standing of the area of concern, such as gender or ethnicity, and ultimately to a decision or commitment to a way of being, say, a female or a Puerto Rican. It is likely that many of the early adolescents whom Brown and Tappan stud-ied, if followed longitudinally, would, in a few years, have a clearer and more stable gender identity, having found ways to assert or express themselves as females that fit their values and goals. Such differences over time are docu-mented by research on ethnic or racial identity (Yip et al., 2006).

As Hurtado and Silva suggest in Chapter Two and Brown and Tappan in Chapter Four, adolescents must exert effort and continue identity work beyond adolescence. There is increasing evidence that identity exploration and reflection persists into young adulthood (Coté, 2006; Phinney, 2006). Chapters One and Six deal with the continuation of identity development in college students. The complex reasoning ability of college students and their wider experience of the world make their identity work more far rang-ing than that of adolescents. In Chapter One, Azmitia, Syed, and Radmacher present longitudinal data showing the evolution in college students' identi-ties over time as they strive to understand and integrate career, ethnic, gen-der, and class identities. Just as at earlier ages, identity options and decisions are influenced by many factors in the college environment, including classes and classmates, and off-campus, including family and friends. Prejudice and discrimination appear here, as they do in earlier developmental periods, as being strong spurs for identity exploration. The interview data provide insight into the complexity of the process as we hear students wrestling with the meanings and implications of their varied experiences for the identity issues they are exploring and attempting to integrate.

In a very different way, Orbe lays out a theoretical framework in Chap-ter Six for understanding identity exploration in college students from a dialectical perspective, that is, in terms of opposing tensions. Although he presents his research in terms of first-generation college students, most of these dialectical challenges are common to college students generally, par-ticularly to those from ethnic minority backgrounds. According to the the-ory, the outcome of managing the stress associated with these tensions is growth, that is, a more complex identity, inclusive of the two poles. This process has clear parallels with Erikson's theory of identity formation (1968), which proposes that individuals experience crises that propel them to explore alternative or competing options regarding key identity issues and to make commitments that allow them to move forward. It is likely, however, that in many areas of identity exploration, there may be more than simply two opposing tensions that need to be resolved.

NEW DIRECTIONS FOR CHILD AND ADOLESCENT DEVELOPMENT • DOI: 10.1002/cd

The previous six chapters in the volume provide varied insights into the question raised in Chapter One: When and how do group identities develop? It is clear, first, that the term *group identity* has different meanings at different stages of development. For young children, identity begins with learning the label used to indicate the groups they belong to. Development consists of gaining understanding of the stability of this group membership over time and of the attributes associated with it. The proximal environment provides the child with varying experiences that convey the salience, signif-icance, and affective tone of the group membership, and these experiences shape the child's developing self-concept as a group member. Throughout childhood, these concepts become more complex and abstract. For gender, we know that the concept becomes less rigid, but little is known about rigidity of other group stereotypes in children.

During adolescence, group identities become a more conscious focus of attention as young people struggle to construct their sense of self as a group member by evaluating the differing messages, images, and feelings about their group. This process is important for all youth, but it is especially salient for those whose group memberships are less highly valued in society, such as ethnic minority groups, the poor, females, or the disabled. As with young children, the context shapes this process in both positive and negative ways. Negative images of one's group can result in children and adolescents not wanting to belong to their group. However, strong ethnic communities (Rosenthal & Hrynevich, 1985; Umaña-Taylor, Bhanot, & Shin, 2006), fam-ily socialization (Umaña-Taylor et al., 2006), and programs highlighting diversity in positive ways (Chapter Two) can help counteract this tendency.

Attending a university provides a context that raises further identity questions as young adults deal with a wide range of new experiences that highlight contrasts between home and school or between themselves and others and try to make decisions for their future. Over the college years, stu-dents show evidence of increasingly complex reasoning and higher levels of integration among various identities.

In summary, at all ages, individuals' understandings of themselves as group members are a product of their cognitive level of understanding of the social world in interaction with the social context to which they are exposed. In spite of the differences in identity formation across age and type of iden-tity, a commonality that transcends these differences is the idea that effort, or identity work, is needed to advance the process of identity formation. At all ages, key factors that propel this process are the contrasts and comparisons that can serve as triggers promoting exploration and growth. A group iden-tity typically includes a sense of what one is not, as well as what one is. The opposite gender or other ethnic groups can serve as foils against which to establish one's own sense of self. Other types of contrasts are important as well—for example, the differences between how one ought to be treated and one's actual treatment in cases of discrimination; the positive feelings about one's group derived from family versus the negative images in the media; and the person one hopes to be in contrast to the stereotypes that may appear to limit those hopes. Individuals need to make considerable effort to achieve some resolution of these contrasting attitudes and experiences.

Descriptions of the development of group identity in broad general strokes can do no more than provide a rudimentary overview of the development of specific group identities. The complexity of identity formation, involving different types of identities and different developmental periods, makes it impossible to use single models or unitary approaches to the topic. Much more research is needed to get a fine-grained picture of the extent to which various group identities show similar or differing developmental patterns and contextual influences. A question of particular interest that cuts across many identities is the role of identity in psychological well-being. In Chapter Three, Lurye, Zosuls, and Ruble highlight the complexity of this question in showing that in children, the relationships among gender identity and adjustment depend on the aspect of identity being considered and the timing of developmental processes. Another question of interest is whether the trajectory of rigidity of gender stereotypes and its impact on adjustment is similar for racial and ethnic stereotypes. A considerable amount of research on this issue has been carried out with different aspects of group identities and different age groups. For example, among adolescents, ethnic affirmation is consistently related to psychological well-being (Phinney, Cantu, & Kurtz, 1997). Clearly, research on group identities is needed to explore which aspects of a given identity, during what developmental periods, and under what conditions, predict psychological adjustment.

Many other questions about similarities and differences in the development of group identities come to mind. How does the influence of factors such as family, peers, social context, and the media on various group identities vary over time and over developmental stages? What are the similarities and differences in the struggle over conflicting dialectical tensions and the process of identity exploration across various group identities? Because of the many interesting questions that need to be studied, research in this area is likely to prove exciting for years to come.

Interdisciplinarity

The second theme of this volume is the idea that the complex processes of identity development can best be understood through interdisciplinary approaches. The term *interdisciplinary* can have different meanings, such as drawing from various theoretical perspectives or using methods from different disciplines. Historically developmental psychology has been more interdisciplinary than most other branches of psychology. Its leading scholars have come from a variety of areas, including social and clinical psychology, anthropology, sociology, education, and counseling. There is also long tradition of using varied methods to study children, including interviews, observation, ethnographies, and experiments.

The value of interdisciplinary approaches can best be realized when different theories and methods are combined in a single study, and this has been much less common in the field. One index of interdisciplinarity is the use of a variety of theoretical perspectives. Azmitia, Syed, and Radmacher point out in Chapter One that many different theories are used in this book. Most evident are theoretical perspectives from developmental psychology, including those of Kohlberg, Erikson, and Gilligan, and from social psychology, particularly the social identity theory of Tajfel. In addition, multicultural education, feminist discourse, sociocultural and ecological theories, and dialectical theory are invoked in some of the chapters. Clearly a complex topic such as identity development can benefit from the insights of scholars from varied backgrounds using different approaches.

However, there has been relatively little research on group identities that is in fact interdisciplinary. Even within the field of psychology, the subdisciplines of developmental and social psychology have functioned as separate disciplines, with different emphases and research questions and little collaboration. Working across disciplinary boundaries poses a number of potential problems. When different theories are invoked, integrating findings or making comparisons among studies is difficult. When theories have very different underlying assumptions, it may be impossible to reconcile them. For example, feminist discourse and postmodern approaches to studying identity development emphasize the uniqueness of individuals and groups, depending on their situation and context, so that generalizations about development are difficult or impossible. In contrast, traditional developmental theories focus on general principles of development that are similar across individuals and groups. It is likely to be difficult for researchers trying to combine these approaches to find common ground.

The difficulty of combining disciplines is also evident in the use of diverse methods. Most researchers favor either qualitative or quantitative methods and are not trained in, or comfortable with, the nonpreferred method. As a result, mixed-method studies are often praised in concept but ignored in practice. In this volume, qualitative methods such as interviews and ethnographies predominate. These methods are particularly valuable when investigating topics that are complex and have not been widely studied, as is the case in identity development. In this volume, the qualitative data illustrate, in ways that would be impossible with quantitative data, how individuals experience and express their identity struggles.

The insights from these studies could be explored by combining two or more methods in the same study. By combining various methods, researchers can determine the extent to which results from different approaches converge to yield similar findings. By combining qualitative and quantitative methods, researchers can enlarge the scope of single-method studies. The rich descriptive data from qualitative studies could be enhanced by the use of quantitative data, such as the frequencies of the themes identified. Among the questions raised by the chapters are these: How many minority college students have thought about the interactions among their identities or are able to articulate the connections they experience among them? In the study of ethnic identity, what percentage of the participants expressed a particular view, such as non–Puerto Ricans wanting to Puerto Rican? Did any non–Puerto Rican adolescents assert a preference for their own group? In the study of girl fighting, how many girls thought females were tougher or defended "fighting like guys"? Even if numbers are small, numerical results can help put qualitative findings in perspective. Similarly, quantitative studies can be illuminated by qualitative data that provide a deeper understanding of the numerical results. The use of several methods requires more training than is generally provided in graduate programs, so researchers need to search out opportunities to learn alternative methods.

Intersectionality

The concept of intersectionality has been developed in greatest depth by theorists concerned with groups that are doubly (or triply) disadvantaged, usually with reference to gender, class, and race or ethnicity, for example, being Black and female. The emphasis in discussions of intersectionality has typically been on issues of power, status, and stigmatization. This topic is explored in depth in Chapter One by Azmitia, Syed, and Radmacher. The examples from their interviews carried out over the four years of college reveal students talking about the interactive effects of their group identities— notably gender, ethnicity, and class—with their personal identities as they wrestle with decisions about choices of majors and careers. For some of these students, their various identities become more integrated over the college years as they become increasingly aware of the way in which these identities together influence their lives.

The other chapters in the volume acknowledge the importance of the interactive effects of multiple identities and the need for including other identities in research focused on just one of them. However, there are few empirical data that cut across identities. These chapters generally illustrate the difficulty of simultaneously studying two or more group identities. Each of the identities studied has different research traditions, paradigms, and measures and, with rare exceptions, has been studied separately. Qualitative studies such as that by Azmitia, Syed, and Radmacher provide a valuable starting point for research combining several types of identity. Their study illustrates the value of qualitative data in providing examples where ethnicity, gender, or class interacts with personal identity.

Quantitative methods could add to our understanding of intersectionality. Some quantitative research on the topic has involved comparisons within samples that can be subdivided according to two overlapping groups, such as ethnicity and gender, to allow comparisons among, say, Black males, white males, Black females, and white females. Other research has looked at similar aspects of two types of identity; for example, Turner and Brown

(2007) examined the centrality of gender and ethnicity in children along with other aspects of the self-concept. To take the study of intersectionality further, studies are needed that assess similar aspects (such as strength of attachment, extent of exploration, or centrality) of two or more identities and then follow participants longitudinally and examine the ways in which these aspects are related to each other and influence the development of each other over time. One could also compare predictors and outcomes for each identity and explore differences in these relationships across ethnicity, gender, and class. Among the major challenges to doing this sort of research would be clearly defining the concepts and developing measures that could be applied across various types of identities.

Conclusion

At an early age, most children become aware of differences among groups of people. This awareness continues to develop and change throughout life and is a major influence on individuals' sense of themselves as group members, that is, their group identity. Group identities, in turn, are central characteristics that shape the lives of individuals and the societies in which they live (Worchel, 1999). In an increasingly diverse and complex world, it is important to understand the varied and interacting processes that explain how people come to make sense of their group identities and the roles of such identities in their lives. The chapters in this volume illustrate some of these processes and lead to some generalizations. Research reported here shows commonalities in developmental processes across identities, including the role of comparison and contrast in promoting identity exploration and the need for identity work on the part of the individual to construct an identity.

Because of the complexity of group identities and the ways in which they interact, group identities cannot be adequately understood individually and from a single perspective. This volume provides an important step in bringing together diverse perspectives in the attempt to make links across different group identities and different developmental periods. Azmitia, Syed, and Radmacher emphasize in Chapter One the ways in which the use of various theoretical perspectives can highlight aspects of identity that might be ignored within a single perspective and can provide explanations of findings that may not be easily interpretable from one approach.

The volume emphasizes the two themes of interdisciplinarity and intersectionality. These ideas are important in making sense of complex phenomena, and the volume makes a strong case for the value of research across identities and disciplines. However, these two themes pose significant challenges for researchers. Most of the studies reported here, while acknowledging the multiplicity of theories and identities, were carried out primarily within one discipline, focused on one type of identity, and used one methodology. These studies raise the question of how this type of research can be broadened to provide deeper understanding of the complex issues involved.

NEW DIRECTIONS FOR CHILD AND ADOLESCENT DEVELOPMENT • DOI: 10.1002/cd

Both developmental and social psychology provide foundational knowledge for advancing the understanding of multiple identities using interdisciplinary and intersectional approaches. The studies in this volume and elsewhere have described the development of some group identities for some populations and some age ranges. However, there are many gaps in the research. Researchers trained within specific disciplines and research traditions have rarely gone outside their own disciplines to expand the understanding of the development of multiple identities.

Studies that can effectively bridge topics and disciplines are best carried out by teams of scholars from different disciplines and approaches. To move the field forward, it would be valuable for researchers from varying backgrounds with a common interest in this area to work together, exchanging and comparing their theoretical orientations, their research goals, and their methodologies, and identifying ways in which their work could inform each other. Within psychology, developmental and social psychologists, who have much in common but have only rarely drawn from each other's work, could work together productively on issues of identity. Ideally, groups of scholars with different perspectives could develop joint projects, using their combined knowledge of diverse theories and methods. However, this type of research is difficult for both personal and institutional reasons. Until such efforts can be undertaken, exposure to a range of theories and approaches, such as one gets from this volume, is a valuable beginning to a more complex understanding of the topic of group identities.

References

Coté, J. (2006). Emerging adulthood as an institutionalized moratorium: Risks and benefits to identity formation. In J. Arnett & J. Tanner (Eds.), *Emerging adults in America: Coming of age in the 21st century* (pp. 85–116). Washington, DC: American Psychological Association.

Cross, W., & Fhagen-Smith, P. (2001). Patterns of African American identity development: A life span perspective. In C. Wijeyesinghe & B. Jackson III (Eds.), *New perspectives on racial identity development: A theoretical and practical anthology* (pp. 243–270). New York: New York University Press.

Erikson, E. (1968). *Identity: Youth and crisis.* New York: Norton.

Pahl, K., & Way, N. (2006). Longitudinal trajectories of ethnic identity among urban Black and Latino adolescents. *Child Development, 77,* 1403–1415.

Phinney, J. (1989). Stages of ethnic identity development in minority group adolescents. *Journal of Early Adolescence, 9,* 34–49.

Phinney, J. (2006). Ethnic identity exploration in emerging adulthood. In J. Arnett & J. Tanner (Eds.), *Emerging adults in America* (pp. 117–134). Washington, DC: American Psychological Association.

Phinney, J., Cantu, C., & Kurtz, D. (1997). Ethnic and American identity as predictors of self-esteem among African American, Latino, and White adolescents. *Journal of Youth and Adolescence, 26,* 165–185.

Quintana, S. (1998). Children's developmental understanding of ethnicity and race. *Applied and Preventive Psychology, 7,* 27–45.

Rosenthal, D., & Hrynevich, C. (1985). Ethnicity and ethnic identity: A comparative study of Greek-, Italian-, and Anglo-Australian adolescents. *International Journal of Psychology, 20,* 723–742.

Ruble, D., Alvarez, J., Bachman, M., Cameron, J., Fuligni, A., & Garcia Coll, C. (2004). The development of a sense of "we": The emergence and implications of children's collective identity. In M. Bennett & F. Sani (Eds.), *The development of the social self* (pp. 29–76). New York: Psychology Press.

Tajfel, H., & Turner, J. (1986). The social identity theory of intergroup behavior. In S. Worchel & W. Austin (Eds.), *Psychology of intergroup relations* (pp. 7–24). Chicago: Nelson-Hall.

Turner, K., & Brown, C. (2007). The centrality of gender and ethnic identities across individuals and contexts. *Social Development, 16,* 700–719.

Umaña-Taylor, A., Bhanot, R., & Shin, N. (2006). Ethnic identity formation during adolescence: The critical role of families. *Journal of Family Issues, 27,* 390–414.

Worchel, S. (1999). *Written in blood: Ethnic identity and the struggle for human harmony.* New York: Worth.

Yip, T., Seaton, E., & Sellers, R. (2006). African American racial identity across the lifespan: Identity status, identity content, and depressive symptoms. *Child Development, 77,* 1504–1517.

JEAN S. PHINNEY is a professor of psychology at California State University-Los Angeles.

INDEX

111

CAD 117 *Attachment in Adolescence: Reflections and New Angles*
Miri Scharf, Ofra Mayseless, Editors
In recent years, the number of empirical studies examining attachment in adolescence has grown considerably, with most focusing on individual differences in attachment security. This volume goes a step further in extending our knowledge and understanding. The physical, cognitive, emotional, and social changes that characterize adolescence invite a closer conceptual look at attachment processes and organization during this period. The chapter authors, leading researchers in attachment in adolescence, address key topics in attachment processes in adolescence. These include issues such as the normative distancing from parents and the growing importance of peers, the formation of varied attachment hierarchies, the changing nature of attachment dynamics from issues of survival to issues of affect regulation, siblings' similarity in attachment representations, individual differences in social information processes in adolescence, and stability and change in attachment representations in a risk sample. Together the chapters provide a compelling discussion of intriguing issues and broaden our understanding of attachment in adolescence and the basic tenets of attachment theory at large.
ISBN: 978-04702-25608

CAD 116 **Linking Parents and Family to Adolescent Peer Relations: Ethnic and Cultural Considerations**
B. Bradford Brown, Nina S. Mounts, Editors
Ethnic and cultural background shapes young people's development and behavior in a variety of ways, including their interactions with family and peers. The intersection of family and peer worlds during childhood has been studied extensively, but only recently has this work been extended to adolescence. This volume of *New Directions for Child and Adolescent Development* highlights new research linking family to adolescent peer relations from a multiethnic perspective. Using qualitative and quantitative research methods, the contributors consider similarities and differences within and between ethnic groups in regard to several issues: parents' goals and strategies for guiding young people to adaptive peer relationships, how peer relationships shape and are shaped by kin relationships, and the specific strategies that adolescents and parents use to manage information about peers or negotiate rules about peer interactions and relationships. Findings emphasize the central role played by sociocultural context in shaping the complex, bidirectional processes that link family members to adolescents' peer social experiences.
ISBN 978-04701-78010

CAD 115 **Conventionality in Cognitive Development: How Children Acquire Shared Representations in Language, Thought, and Action**
Chuck W. Kalish, Mark A. Sabbagh, Editors
An important part of cognitive development is coming to think in culturally normative ways. Children learn the right names for objects, proper functions for tools, appropriate ways to categorize, and the rules for games. In each of these cases, what makes a given practice normative is not naturally given. There is not necessarily any objectively better or worse way to do any of these things. Instead, what makes them correct is that people agree on how they should be done, and each of these practices therefore has an important conventional basis. The chapters in this volume highlight the fact that successful participation in practices of language, cognition, and play depends on children's ability to acquire representations that other members of their social worlds share. Each of these domains poses problems of identifying normative standards and achieving coordination across agents. This volume brings together scholars from

diverse areas in cognitive development to consider the psychological mechanisms supporting the use and acquisition of conventional knowledge.
ISBN 978-07879-96970

CAD 114 **Respect and Disrespect: Cultural and Developmental Origins**
David W. Schwalb, Barbara J. Schwalb, Editors
Respect enables children and teenagers to value other people, institutions, traditions, and themselves. Disrespect is the agent that dissolves positive relationships and fosters hostile and cynical relationships. Unfortunately, parents, educators, children, and adolescents in many societies note with alarm a growing problem of disrespect and a decline in respect for self and others. Is this disturbing trend a worldwide problem? To answer this question, we must begin to study the developmental and cultural origins of respect and disrespect. Five research teams report that respect and disrespect are influenced by experiences in the family, school, community, and, most importantly, the broader cultural setting. The chapters introduce a new topic area for mainstream developmental sciences that is relevant to the interests of scholars, educators, practitioners, and policymakers.
ISBN 978-07879-95584

CAD 113 **The Modernization of Youth Transitions in Europe**
Manuela du Bois-Reymond, Lynne Chisholm, Editors
This compelling volume focuses on what it is like to be young in the rapidly changing, enormously diverse world region that is early 21st century Europe. Designed for a North American readership interested in youth and young adulthood, *The Modernization of Youth Transitions in Europe* provides a rich fund of theoretical insight and empirical evidence about the implications of contemporary modernization processes for young people living, learning, and working across Europe. Chapters have been specially written for this volume by well-known youth sociologists; they cover a wide range of themes against a shared background of the reshaping of the life course and its constituent phases toward greater openness and contigency. New modes of learning accompany complex routes into employment and career under rapidly changing labor market conditions and occupational profiles, while at the same time new family and lifestyle forms are developing alongside greater intergenerational responsibilities in the face of the retreat of the modern welfare state. The complex patterns of change for today's young Europeans are set into a broader framework that analyzes the emergence and character of European youth research and youth policy in recent years.
ISBN 978-07879-88890

CAD 112 **Rethinking Positive Adolescent Female Sexual Development**
Lisa M. Diamond, Editor
This volume provides thoughtful and diverse perspectives on female adolescent sexuality. These perspectives integrate biological, cultural, and interpersonal influences on adolescent girls' sexuality, and highlight the importance of using multiple methods to investigate sexual ideation and experience. Traditional portrayals cast adolescent females as sexual gatekeepers whose primary task is to fend off boys' sexual overtures and set aside their own sexual desires in order to reduce their risks for pregnancy and sexually transmitted diseases. Yet an increasing number of thoughtful and constructive critiques have challenged this perspective, arguing for more sensitive, in-depth, multimethod investigations into the positive meanings of sexuality for adolescent girls that will allow us to conceptualize (and, ideally, advocate for) healthy sexual-developmental trajectories. Collectively, authors of this volume take up

this movement and chart exciting new directions for the next generation of developmental research on adolescent female sexuality.
ISBN 978-07879-87350

CAD111 **Family Mealtime as a Context for Development and Socialization**
Reed W. Larson, Angela R. Wiley, Kathryn R. Branscomb, Editors
This issue examines the impact of family mealtime on the psychological development of young people. In the popular media, family mealtime is often presented as a vital institution for the socialization and development of young people, but also as one that is "going the way of the dinosaur." Although elements such as fast food and TV have become a part of many family mealtimes, evidence is beginning to suggest that mealtimes can also provide rich opportunities for children's and adolescents' development. While what happens at mealtimes varies greatly among families, an outline of the forms and functions of mealtimes is beginning to emerge from this research. In this issue, leading mealtime researchers from the fields of history, cultural anthropology, psycholinguistics, psychology, and nutrition critically review findings from each of their disciplines, giving primary focus on family mealtimes in the United States. The authors in this issue examine the history of family mealtimes, describe contemporary mealtime practices, elucidate the differing transactional processes that occur, and evaluate evidence on the outcomes associated with family mealtimes from children and adolescents.
ISBN 978-07879-85776

CAD 110 **Leaks in the Pipeline to Math, Science, and Technology Careers**
Janis E. Jacobs, Sandra D. Simpkins, Editors
Around the world, the need for highly trained scientists and technicians remains high, especially for positions that require employees to have a college degree and skills in math, science, and technology. The pipeline into these jobs begins in high school, but many "leaks" occur before young people reach the highly educated workforce needed to sustain leadership in science and technology. Students drop out of the educational pipeline in science and technology at alarming rates at each educational transition beginning in high school, but women and ethnic minority youth drop out at a faster rate. Women and minorities are consistently underrepresented in science and engineering courses and majors. They account for a small portion of the work force in high-paying and more innovative jobs that require advanced degrees. This schism between the skills necessary in our ever-changing economy and the skill set that most young adults acquire is troubling. It leads us to ask the question that forms the basis for this issue: Why are adolescents and young adults, particularly women and minorities, opting out of the math, science, and technology pipeline? The volume addresses gender and ethnic differences in the math, science, and technology pipeline from multiple approaches, including theoretical perspectives, a review of the work in this field, presentation of findings from four longitudinal studies, and a discussion of research implications given the current educational and economic climate.
ISBN 978-07879-83932

CAD 109 **New Horizons in Developmental Theory and Research**
Lene Arnett Jensen, Reed W. Larson, Editors
This inaugural issue by the new editors-in-chief brings together a group of cutting-edge developmental scholars who each report on promising new lines of theory and research within their specialty areas. Their essays cover a selection of important topics including emotion-regulation, family socialization, friendship, self, civic engagement, media, and culture. In the succinct, engag-

ing essays, all authors provide thought-provoking views of the horizons in the field.
ISBN 978-07879-83413

CAD 108 **Changing Boundaries of Parental Authority During Adolescence**
Judith Smetena, Editor
This volume describes research focusing on changes in different dimensions of parenting and conceptions of parental authority during adolescence. The seven chapters illuminate the dimensions of parenting that change (or remain stable) over the course of adolescence. The chapters also ighlight the importance of considering variations in parenting accoding to the different domains of adolescents' lives, their relationships to the development of responsibility automony, and how these are influenced by socioeconomic status, culture, and ethnicity. Thus, the chapters in this volume provide new directions for conceptualizing variations in parenting over the second decade of life and their implicaions for adolescent adjustment and well-being. The authors point to the need for developmentally sensitive models of parenting that consider changes within domains over time, their influence on adolescent development and functioning, and potential asynchronies between parents and adolescents.
ISBN 978-07879-81921

CAD 107 **The Experience of Close Friendship in Adolescence**
Niobe Way, Jill V. Hamm, Editors
In this issue, we present findings from four studies that employed qualitative methodology to gain insight into the how and the why of close friendships. How do adolescents experience trust and intimacy in their friendships? Why are these relational experiences critical for emotional adjustment? And how does the social and cultural context shape the ways in which adolescents experience their close friendships? The studies reveal the ways in which adolescents from diverse cultural backgrounds speak about their close friendships and the individual and contextual factors that shape and are shaped by their experiences of close friendships.
ISBN 978-07879-80573

CAD 106 **Social and Self Process Underlying Math and Science Achievement**
Heather Bouchey, Cynthia Winston, Editors
In general, America's students are not faring well in science and mathematics. The chapters in this volume employ novel conceptual and empirical approaches to investigate how social and individual factors interact to effect successful math and science achievement. Each of the chapters is solidly grounded in theory and provides new insight concerning the integration of student-level and contextual influences. Inclusion of youth from diverse socioeconomic and ethnic backgrounds is a salient feature of the volume.
ISBN 978-07879-79164

CAD 105 **Human Technogenesis: Cultural Pathways Through the Information Age**
Dinesh Sharma, Editor
The technologically driven information economy is reshaping everyday human behavior and sociocultural environments. Yet our paradigms for understanding human development within a cultural framework are guided by traditional and dichotomous ideas about the social world (for example, individualism-collectivism, egocentric-sociocentric, modern-traditional, Western-Non-Western). As the impact of information technologies permeates all aspects of our lives, research in human development and psychology must face the digitally, connected social environments as its laboratory, filled

with naturally occurring experiments, whether it is the speed at which we now communicate in the home or workplace, the far-reaching access children have to a wide array of information previously unavailable, or the vicarious anonymity with which we are able to participate in each other's lives through the new media tools. The chapters in this volume claim that the recent wave of innovation and adaptation to information technologies, giving rise to a new form of "human technogenesis," is fundamentally transforming our everyday interactions and potentially reconstructing the nature and process of human development. Human technogenesis is the constructive process of individual and sociocultural innovation and adaptation to the everyday interactions with information technologies, which significantly affects the developing and the developed mind.
ISBN 978-07879-77795

CAD 104 *Culture and Developing Selves: Beyond Dichotomization*
Michael F. Mascolo, Jin Li, Editors
The distinction between individualism and collectivism (I-C) has been useful in understanding differences in the world's cultures and the developing selves that they spawn. From this view, within Individualist (most North American and Western-European) cultures, individuals develop a sense of self as separate, autonomous, and independent of others. In contrast, collectivist cultures (for example, many Asian cultures) place primary value on group orientation, the goals and needs of others, and readiness to cooperate. However, despite its utility, the I-C dimension can obscure an analysis of the complexity of selves that develop in individualist and collectivist cultures. Individuality and interiority are represented in selves that develop within cultures considered collectivistic; conversely; selves in individualist cultures are defined through relations with others. The contributors to this volume examine the multiplicity of developing selfhood that exists within and between cultures. In so doing, the contributors examine the coexistence of self-cultivation and social obligation among the Chinese, the coexistence of deep spiritual interiority and social duty in urban India, changing patterns of identity in immigrant families, and how autonomy functions in the service of social relations among American adolescents. It is argued that individuality and connectedness cannot exist independent of each other. Although there are dramatic differences in how they are constructed, individual and communal dimensions of selfhood must be represented in some form in selves that develop in all cultures.
ISBN 978-07879-76262

CAD 103 *Connections Between Theory of Mind and Sociomoral Development*
Jodie A. Baird, Bryan W. Sokol
The heightened attention to research on theory of mind is due in large part to the shared intuition that this core aspect of development must have important consequences for, and connections with, children's evolving social competence. This seems particularly true for the moral domain, where a psychological, or inward, focus is often taken to be a constitutive feature of what distinguishes moral actions from other kinds of behavior. Unfortunately, the theory-of-mind enterprise has largely failed to capitalize on this fundamental connection between mental life and morality, and, as a result, it has been effectively cut off from the study of sociomoral development. The chapters in this volume represent different, though complementary, attempts to bridge the gap that exists between these research traditions. Two central questions are addressed. First, what is the impact of children's conceptions of the mind on their moral judgements? Second, does children's mental state under-

standing influence the moral quality of their own behavior? In the concluding chapters, prominent scholars from both the theory-of-mind literature and the moral development domain comment on the efforts being made to link these research traditions and offer suggestions for future inquiry.
ISBN 978-07879-74404

CAD 102 **Enemies and the Darker Side of Peer Relations**
Ernest V. Hodges, Noel A. Card, Editors
The darker side of peer relations is subject that has been largely ignored by researchers. This volume begins the much-needed theoretical and empirically based explorations of the factors involved in the foremation, maintenance, and impact of enemies and other mutual antipathies. Using diverse samples, the chapter authors provide an empirically based exposition of factors relevant to the formation and maintenance of these relations, as well as their developmental impact. Both distal (for example, attachment styles with parents, community violence exposure) and proximal (for example, perceptions of enemies' behavior, social structure of the peer group) factors related to inimical relations are explored, and the developmental sequelaw (for example, affective, behavioral, interpersonal) of having enemies are examined with concurrent and longitudinal designs.
ISBN 978-07879-72721

CAD 101 **Person-Centered Approaches to Studying Development in Context**
Stephen C. Peck, Robert W. Roeser, Editors
This volume introduces readers to theoretical and methodological discussions, along with empirical illustrations, of using pattern-centered analyses in studying development in context. Pattern-centered analytic techniques refer to a family of research tools that identify patterns or profiles of variables within individuals and thereby classify individuals into homogeneous subgroups based on their similarity of profile. These techniques find their theoretical foundation in holistic, developmental systems theories in which notions of organization, process dynamics, interactions and transactions, context, and life course development are focal. The term *person-centered* is used to contrast with the traditional emphasis on variables; the term *pattern-centered* is used to extend the principles of person-centered approaches to other levels of analysis (for example, social context). Contributors present the theoretical foundations of pattern-centered analytic techniques, describe specific tools that may be of use to developmentalists interested in using such techniques and provide four empirical illustrations of their use in relation to educational achievement and attainments, aggressive behavior and social popularity, and alcohol use during the childhood and adolescent periods.
ISBN 978-07879-71694

CAD 100 **Exploring Cultural Conceptions of the Transitions to Adulthood**
Jeffrey Jensen Arnett, Editor
The transition to adulthood has been studied for decades in terms of transition events such as leaving home, finishing education, and entering marriage and parenthood, but only recently have studies examined the conceptions of young people themselves on what it means to become an adult. The goal of this volume is to extend the study of conceptions of adulthood to a wider range of cultures. The chapters in this volume examine conceptions of adulthood among Israelis, Argentines, American Mormons, Germans, Canadians, and three American ethnic minority groups. There is a widespread emphasis across cultures on individualistic criteria for adulthood, but each culture has

been found to emphasize culturally distinctive criteria as well. This volume represents a beginning in research on cultural conceptions of the transition to adulthood and points the way to a broad range of opportunities for future investigation.
ISBN 978-07879-69813

CAD 99 **Examining Adolescent Leisure Time Across Cultures: Developmental Opportunities and Risks**
Suman Verma, Reed W. Larson, Editors
Adolescence worldwide is a life period of role restructuring and social learning. Free-time activities provide opportunities to experiment with roles and develop new adaptive strategies and other interpersonal skills that have an impact on development, socialization, and the transition to adulthood. Leisure provides a rich context in which adolescents can gain control over their attentional processes and learn from relationships with peers, but it also has potential costs, such as involvement in deviant and risk behaviors. To gain deeper insight into the developmental opportunities and risks that adolescents experience in their free time, this volume explores adolescents' daily leisure experience across countries. Each chapter describes the sociocultural contexts in which adolescents live, along with a profile of free-time activities. Collectively, the chapters highlight the differences and similarities between cultures; how family, peers, and wider social factors influence the use of free time; which societies provide more freedom and at what costs; and how adolescents cope with restricted degrees of freedom and with what consequences on their mental health and well-being.
ISBN 978-07879-68366

NEW DIRECTIONS FOR CHILD & ADOLESCENT DEVELOPMENT
Order Form
SUBSCRIPTIONS AND SINGLE ISSUES

DISCOUNTED BACK ISSUES:

Use this form to receive **20% off** all back issues of New Directions for Child & Adolescent Development. All single issues priced at **$23.20** (normally $29.00)

TITLE	ISSUE NO.	ISBN
_____	_____	_____
_____	_____	_____
_____	_____	_____

Call 888-378-2537 or see mailing instructions below. When calling, mention the promotional code, JB7ND, to receive your discount.
For a complete list of issues, please visit www.josseybass.com/go/ndcad

SUBSCRIPTIONS: *(1 year, 4 issues)*

☐ New Order   ☐ Renewal

U.S.	☐ Individual: $85	☐ Institutional: $258
Canada/Mexico	☐ Individual: $85	☐ Institutional: $298
All Others	☐ Individual: $109	☐ Institutional: $332

Call 888-378-2537 or see mailing and pricing instructions below. Online subscriptions are available at www.interscience.wiley.com.

Copy or detach page and send to:
John Wiley & Sons, Journals Dept, 5th Floor
989 Market Street, San Francisco, CA 94103-1741
Order Form can also be faxed to: 888-481-2665

Issue/Subscription Amount: $ _____	**SHIPPING CHARGES:**
Shipping Amount: $ _____	SURFACE Domestic Canadian
(for single issues only—subscription prices include shipping)	First Item $5.00 $6.00
Total Amount: $ _____	Each Add'l Item $3.00 $1.50

(No sales tax for U.S. subscriptions. Canadian residents, add GST for subscription orders. Individual rate subscriptions must be paid by personal check or credit card. Individual rate subscriptions may not be resold as library copies.)

☐ Payment enclosed (U.S. check or money order only. All payments must be in U.S. dollars.)

☐ VISA   ☐ MC   ☐ Amex # _____ Exp. Date _____

Card Holder Name _____ Card Issue # _____

Signature_____ Day Phone _____

☐ Bill Me (U.S. institutional orders only. Purchase order required.)

Purchase order # _____
Federal Tax ID13559302   GST 89102 8052

Name_____

Address _____

Phone _____ E-mail _____

JB7ND

NEW DIRECTIONS FOR CHILD AND ADOLESCENT DEVELOPMENT IS NOW AVAILABLE ONLINE AT WILEY INTERSCIENCE

What is Wiley InterScience?

Wiley InterScience is the dynamic online content service from John Wiley & Sons delivering the full text of over 300 leading scientific, technical, medical, and professional journals, plus major reference works, the acclaimed Current Protocols laboratory manuals, and even the full text of select Wiley print books online.

What are some special features of Wiley InterScience?

Wiley Interscience Alerts is a service that delivers table of contents via e-mail for any journal available on Wiley InterScience as soon as a new issue is published online.
EarlyView is Wiley's exclusive service presenting individual articles online as soon as they are ready, even before the release of the compiled print issue. These articles are complete, peer-reviewed, and citable.
CrossRef is the innovative multi-publisher reference linking system enabling readers to move seamlessly from a reference in a journal article to the cited publication, typically located on a different server and published by a different publisher.

How can I access Wiley InterScience?

Visit http://www.interscience.wiley.com.

Guest Users can browse Wiley InterScience for unrestricted access to journal tables of contents and article abstracts, or use the powerful search engine.
Registered Users are provided with a *Personal Home Page* to store and manage customized alerts, searches, and links to favorite journals and articles. Additionally, Registered Users can view free online sample issues and preview selected material from major reference works.
Licensed Customers are entitled to access full-text journal articles in PDF, with select journals also offering full-text HTML.

How do I become an Authorized User?

Authorized Users are individuals authorized by a paying Customer to have access to the journals in Wiley InterScience. For example, a university that subscribes to Wiley journals is considered to be the Customer.
Faculty, staff, and students authorized by the university to have access to those journals in Wiley InterScience are Authorized Users. Users should contact their library for information on which Wiley journals they have access to in Wiley InterScience.